Keys to Lasting Transformation

DR. JANETTE MARIE FREEMAN

Why Did This Happen to Me Again?
By Dr. Janette Marie Freeman

© Janette Marie Freeman, 2005
Why Did This Happen to Me Again?

Second Edition 2019

Senior Editor
Barbara Foley

Editors
Brad Fregger
Katherine Bishop
Kathleen Magor

Cover Design and Production
Amy Nottingham-Martin

All rights reserved. No part of this book may be reproduced or utilized in any form or by any means, electronic or mechanical, including photocopying, recording, or by an information storage and retrieval system, without written permission from the author

WHY DID THIS HAPPEN TO ME AGAIN?

To my three children Athena, Arielle, and Peter…

May you always know how much I love you. You are the Light.

CONTENTS

Introduction   *1*

CHAPTER ONE
Discover the Key to Greater Happiness   9

    An Autobiography in Five Chapters 11
    Unleash your freedom 12
    Sleep your way to greater success 15
    Simplify and discover your power 18

CHAPTER TWO
Build a Strong Foundation   21

    Eliminate weak beliefs and build strong ones 22
    Overcome your early programming 23
    Understand how old beliefs operate and new ones form 25
    Claim your spiritual freedom 31
    Know with whom and what you identify 37

CHAPTER THREE
Identify and Abolish Limiting Beliefs   41

    Assess and identify your personal beliefs 41
    Question your limited beliefs, gain understanding 43
    Unravel the seven core beliefs that undermine your success ... 46

CHAPTER FOUR
Discover the Secrets to Living in Bliss — 63

    Stop surviving and start thriving 64

    Use these five powerful tools to raise consciousness 76

CHAPTER FIVE
Break the Cycle — 79

    Welcome your pain and convert it to power 80

    Embrace the transforming process 87

    Reprogram your belief system 89

    Choose to suffer or choose to be free 91

    Reprogramming Worksheet 92

    Accept responsibility for your emotions, transform your life 94

CHAPTER SIX
Simplify Your Meditation Practice for Lasting Transformation — 97

    Meditate to bring freedom from past beliefs 97

    Ten measurable benefits of meditation 99

    Easy meditation practices anyone can do 101

    Tips for successful meditation 103

CHAPTER SEVEN
Make It Easy by Making It a Habit — 105

    Use repetition to be happy and free 105

    Three easy practices that work every time 106

    What we say to ourselves can set us free or hold us in bondage 109

    Praise and honor yourself 110

    Twenty surefire and easy ways to transform your life 112

CHAPTER EIGHT
Unlock Greater Possibilities — 117

Explore and discover your innate genius 117
Dare to dream in order to have a dream come true 118
Unleash the fourteen-hour commitment in your life and win 122

CHAPTER NINE
Revolutionary Results with Sleep-Repetition—THE EASY WAY — 127

It's fast, easy, and effective 127
Starting the practice of sleep-learning 130
Proven secrets can do wonders for children 132
Use sleep-repetition to make you happy, healthy, and wealthy 135

CHAPTER TEN
Lasting transformation Is Yours — 137

Be the master of your fate 137
Know who are you and with whom you identify 140
Take responsibility, muster courage, and create joy 143
We are more than our stories, our histories, and the roles we play 144

Affirmations   *147*
Reading List   *165*
About the Author   *167*

INTRODUCTION

And this book began ...

Just a year ago, I looked around the chaotic baggage claim area at the airport on one of the busiest days of the year, the day after Christmas. Confusion was rampant and anxiety filled the air. It was late in the day, and exhausted children screamed and fought over toys while tired, frustrated mothers did their best to corral them. I watched as the crushed boxes scattered the Christmas treasures, and the luggage with the broken zipper went around and around on the baggage carousel. There was a palpable heaviness in the air as people were concerned with their possessions, schedules, demands, and delays.

As I sat waiting for my husband to get our luggage—numbed and tired from my travels—I found myself staring blankly at the scene before me. Then the view began to take on a sharper quality, with certain images coming into focus. There was a moment of indescribable clarity—a flash of insight—as delicious yet daunting questions took me deeper into Reality than I had gone for a very long time. I saw beyond the physical plane for only a flash, but in that brief instant my destiny became clear. A second seemed to last a lifetime, and in that second I realized:

> *The world we live in is literally a creation of our innermost thoughts and beliefs.*
> *Our lives can be changed, simply by a consistent change of thought.*

From that most powerful and potent moment in time, I knew that it was the work of my life to do what I could to awaken people to their creative natures, their divine potentials, by taking my insights and knowledge and sharing them in the simplest way I know.

Right now in my life, I do feel on top of the world. I'm living my dreams and busy dreaming new dreams to live. I work as a minister, teacher, speaker, and real estate investor. I live in a beautiful home; I travel; I enjoy wonderful children; and I have a supportive, loving husband. I love my work and I am surrounded by people whom I love and who love me. I'm always on the edge of my next exciting adventure, and I love it that way. My spiritual life is rich and fulfilling, and I am at peace with myself. But this life of mine is just beginning, and I have so much more to do, to accomplish, and to experience.

Life wasn't always like this for me. There was a time, not so long ago, when the dream was little more than a distant speck in my hopeless heart. As a young thirty-something woman, I was miserable: life held very little hope, and the day-to-day experiences carried with them a struggle to survive, let alone thrive. I was a single mother with three young children. Struggling to support my young family, I felt trapped in jobs that didn't feed my heart with joy and in relationships that continued to validate my feelings of unworthiness. Yet, I knew this wasn't what life was supposed to look like. I knew, in the depths of my being, that I could live a different life. My soul screamed for release and renewal.

> I was surprised to hear, "Are you Janette Rose? The phone is for you," as I sat in the beauty salon with half my hair in perm rods.
>
> "Yes, I'm Janette," I tentatively replied. I saw the dread in her eyes as she slowly handed me the phone, and I knew something was wrong, terribly wrong.
>
> "Ms. Rose, this is the emergency room. I'm sorry, your son

and fiancé are here and they have been in a car accident." At that moment, life seemed to stand still.

> I had been dating Bob on and off for a couple of years. It had been a long-distance relationship; he lived in Florida while I lived in Southern California. We had spent only the last couple of months together. I was tired of being single, tired of doing everything, tired of caring for the needs of my three children, ages eight, eleven, and thirteen. I was tired of being broke, exhausted, and worn out. I wanted to be saved. Bob told me everything I wanted to hear.

My eight-year-old son Peter and my fiancé Bob had dropped me off to get my hair permed an hour before, with only two weeks to go before our wedding. They were off for a little "bonding" time.

"Don't worry, they're okay," the E.R. nurse reported. "Your son has some kind of hand injury. Your fiancé has a few scratches but he will be released. Your son is waiting for the doctor to look at his hand."

> Peter did not particularly like Bob. None of the kids did. They were suspicious of him; I just wanted it to work. Funny how sometimes kids have better instincts than we do.

On this particular Saturday afternoon after dropping me off at the salon, Bob had taken Peter to the Chevrolet dealership to test-drive a brand new Corvette. Surely an eight-year-old boy would like the speed and thrill of driving a hot sports car. But maybe not when he was put on the salesman's lap in the front passenger seat of the low-lying T-top. Bob took the canyon curves at over 80 miles an hour, and flipped the car over five times, landing upside down. The skin on Peter's hand was ripped from his palm, and a mass of flesh, blood supply, and nerves was torn from his wrist.

When I walked into the emergency room and saw my sweet, scared little boy lying in shock on the gurney, I let out a scream and ran over to him. When he saw me, he began to whimper. He looked white and clammy with fear and appeared dazed and confused. The doctor quickly told me not to look at his hand, which was covered with a cloth. After I caught my breath, I asked him, "Why not?" He began to tell me the extent of the injury of Peter's right wrist. As the doctor walked away, I lifted the cloth. I could not fight back the tears as the reality of my son's injury slapped me in the face.

> Our wedding was two weeks away. I had sent out the invitations and thought all was in place. We had booked the top floor of a beautiful tower restaurant in Ventura, California, planned the menu, ordered the dress and flowers, and reserved the minister. With the wedding came the new house (already in escrow), the car, and the money; it would all be better soon. Of course, I had placed the deposit on the dress and paid for the invitations and the incidentals myself; he was waiting for a large deal to close, due to happen at any time.

Peter would need a specialist and UCLA had the best. His hand needed immediate reconstruction work, and arrangements were made for the ambulance transport. An hour later we were at UCLA Medical Center, meeting with the Director of Orthopedics and Plastic Surgery, Dr. Neil Jones, who was one of the area's finest hand specialists. This was the first of several surgeries and the long and drawn-out physical therapy that Peter would endure.

> I had overlooked Bob's inconsistencies because I so wanted to believe. I wanted to believe that he would take care of me and the kids. I wanted to believe that we could live in a beautiful home. I wanted to believe that the kids would have all that they needed. I wanted to believe that he loved me with all his heart and would do anything for me. I wanted to believe that he loved my kids and would take good care of us.

The first one-and-a-half-week stay in the children's ward at UCLA was not an easy time; yet in some strange way, it provided Peter and me an experience of togetherness I will never forget. I stayed with him nearly non-stop during this traumatic time. It would be years before he could go to the dentist or any doctor's appointment without breaking out in a total panic.

The pain of the missing skin was unbearable at times, particularly when they had to cleanse and soak his hand three times a day. They also took skin and tissue from his back and surgically placed it on his wrist, replacing the blood supply and tissue. Later they would remove nerves from his leg through an intense and revolutionary microsurgery, replacing the lost nerves in his hand.

Miraculously, he would regain the full use and feeling in his hand in the long months of therapy that followed.

> One week before the wedding we returned home from the hospital. I don't remember much about the days that followed our arrival home except Peter's excruciatingly painful soaking and washing of his hand. I do remember getting the call though, on the day before the wedding, that the check Bob wrote for the balance on my dress had bounced. And then there was the call from the restaurant that the reception was cancelled because of the bounced check they had also received. There was no escrow on the house. It seemed that the house of cards was about to come crashing down. It was time for me to wake up. It was time to take back my power.

Thank God for family. They thought that they had come for a wedding; instead it was to pick me up, shake me off, and remind me who I was. They were my backbone when I forgot where mine was, and they helped me not get sucked back into the lies of a desperate man.

> This was not an easy recovery, not for Peter and not for me. Not only had I spent more than I should have in wedding costs, but Bob had left me with over $2,000 in phone charges and his bounced checks accumulated over $300 in bank charges. With the amount of work I missed

> because of Peter's accident, I was in dire financial straits. We moved out of our three-bedroom condo in Thousand Oaks, and thankfully, because of a good friend, we moved into a one-bedroom basement apartment in someone's home. We were starting over.
>
> I learned a deep and powerful lesson. I would rely upon me. I would build a new life and I would not blame Bob. I would accept that my neediness and desperation had made me blind. I would grow and learn, and I would get stronger. We would not fail; we would rise above this. Peter's hand would heal; that was the only alternative in my mind. He would not be handicapped by this experience, not physically or emotionally. And neither would I. What doesn't kill you will make you stronger, right? I had heard that.

The great thing about being really miserable, as opposed to slightly and tolerably miserable, is that it forces you to do something, anything. You're willing to open up to new possibilities because you can't tolerate your current reality for another minute! So that was where I was. Although I didn't know it at the time, it was a good thing. It forced me to look deep within and choose to recreate my life, leading ultimately to my discovery of the power of repetition of positive affirmations—and other life-changing processes for manifesting greater happiness and success.

Why do I teach the power of repetition? Because it worked for me and it continues to work for others. I have worked with thousands of people and have found the KEY to assist people in their own transformation. It is so simple that it is often overlooked: *that KEY is repetition.*

I'm not talking about a diet of affirmations that we get bored with after a while; I'm talking about developing repetitive practices that change our lifestyles and belief systems. With the realization that our repetitive thought practices are creating our reality, we begin to understand that we must create new thought patterns if we want to have a change of experience. *The input determines the output. Thought creates reality.*

Experiences are created not just from conscious thought but from subconscious thought as well. That's where it gets tricky. In this book, you will learn the skills needed to easily recognize when your subconscious beliefs are triggered, so that you can recognize them and reprogram them.

You will learn how your subconscious beliefs have been directing your life; creating painful relationships; holding you in fear, insecurity, and depression; forming limiting resources; and holding you in an overall sense of hopelessness.

This does not have to be your life! You can learn how to recognize your disruptive patterns and begin to repetitively reprogram your own belief systems in order to create lasting change and transformation. Let your journey to a new life begin this very moment.

CHAPTER ONE

DISCOVER THE KEY TO GREATER HAPPINESS

Do you wonder why your efforts at personal transformation don't seem to last?

Do you get excited about some new idea, but after a while you slip right back into your old patterns?

Do you get turned on by a new vision, dream, or plan, just to have it cremated by the voices of fear and trepidation inside your own head?

Does the religion you grew up in no longer work for you, but you don't dare change for fear of what family members might say?

How many of your dreams, desires, and hopes have been secretly dashed to destruction in the darkest recesses of your mind before they even had a chance to take root?

If you're anything like I was, something in you *knows* that there must be more to life than the day-to-day struggle to survive. There is an urge for greater expression in you; you've seen it, you've tasted it, and you've even made decisions to move towards it. But that voice in your head convinces you that you're crazy.

You've read a lot, you've tried meditating, you've tried affirmations and attended workshops, seminars, and classes. You know that your attitudes play a part in your life, and you've tried desperately to make some headway in your happiness quotient. And then it happens once again: the same old relationship challenges with a new partner, the same difficult-person scenario at work, the same response that triggers the same familiar pain, and you ask yourself, *Why did this happen to me again?*

> As I skim through my journals, I see how, over and over, I have written my dreams, my affirmations, my hurts, and my disappointments. I have decided over and over again that I would attract a wonderful man in my life. And yet, as I look over the past few weeks, I see this new relationship is the same. He is not available. I thought he was. He even said he was. I am tempted to scream and cry out, "Why again, Lord? Why can't I get it? Why can't I see it? I should have known better! Why did this happen again?" I am reminded that the source of my habits runs deep and I surrender again. I will choose again. I must take responsibility for what I attract, and I must agree *again* to let go of my fear of commitment and intimacy. I do this without judgment or blame for myself or others. I am lovable and worthy just the way I am. My presence is enough. It's okay if I'm not perfect and I can allow others to see me. I can be open and I am safe.

I love the following poem and share it with all my students, because in such a clear and simple way it shows how we must acknowledge the part we play in attracting any circumstances into our lives. Until we do so, we keep repeating the same experiences over and over. We begin to free ourselves from the carousel of repeated experiences as we begin to examine the belief systems that are creating our reality.

An Autobiography in Five Chapters
by Portia Nelson

Chapter 1
  I walk down the street.
  There is a deep hole in the sidewalk.
  I fall in.
  I am lost ... I am helpless.
  It isn't my fault.
  It takes forever to find a way out.

Chapter 2
  I walk down the same street.
  There is a deep hole in the sidewalk.
  I pretend I don't see it.
  I fall in, again.
  I can't believe I am in this same place.
  It isn't my fault.
  It still takes a long time to get out.

Chapter 3
  I walk down the same street.
  There is a deep hole in the sidewalk.

I see it is there.
I fall in ... it's a habit ... but now my eyes are open.
I know where I am.
It is my fault.
I get out immediately.

Chapter 4
I walk down the same street.
There is a deep hole in the sidewalk.
I walk around it.

Chapter 5
I walk down a different street.

Unleash your freedom

There is a huge leap in our personal growth, evolution, and freedom when we can take responsibility for our feelings and experiences in life and see them as road maps to self-discovery.

Our belief systems are the brick and mortar of our lives. When they're strong and supportive, they support life choices and actions that are also strong and supportive. When our beliefs are weak and degrading, we tend to see life through those eyes, attracting opportunities to prove ourselves weak and degraded. Until we have a lasting change in our internal belief systems, we seldom see lasting change in our lives. *Why settle for misery when you can be happy?* A strong foundation of supportive beliefs can set you free to live the life of your dreams.

In order to have a lasting transformation, you must experience a change of beliefs at the subconscious level. Although this book will help you get in touch with when and where you got your early beliefs, it is more important that you now establish new beliefs that will assist you in attracting the life you desire. You may never determine the origin of some of your beliefs, but that doesn't stop you from establishing new beliefs. You do this by being exposed to and accepting new ideas *repetitively*. This does not happen with one or two affirmations; it happens when you outweigh your limiting beliefs with positive beliefs.

This book is written for the millions of people who are interested in personal and spiritual growth but are exhausted by their failed efforts. It is for those readers who wonder why their efforts don't seem to last. They get excited by some new idea but after a while slip right back into old patterns. Following through on the new idea can just seem like too much work. They want something that is easier to do, that fits into their busy lifestyle, and that is effective. They want to be encouraged and nurtured, and they need motivation to look above the negativity they see all around them.

The power of repetition is mentioned in one form or another in most self-help books, religious texts, even sports-training and business manuals. They all say the same thing: "You must have a continuous influx of positive input in order to experience a lasting change in life."

Yes, this is true; however, up until now, no book has made repetition its primary focus, reinforcing the necessity of decisive repetition in a person's life. "We are what we think about most," has been taught, preached, and written about for thousands of years. Unconscious thought practices have produced the troubled world we see around us. Conscious thought practices will produce the world we want to see and experience.

Most of everyone's pains and failures in life are simply a result of unhealthy beliefs. Those beliefs can be changed, and this book will show you how to recognize beliefs that cause pain and replace them with beliefs that bring joy and freedom. It is as simple as that. Positive repetition in its many forms can radically transform one's life from painful to joyful, limited to abundant, diseased to healthy, and lonely to loved. ***You can change your beliefs and you can change your life!***

You see, we are creative beings. I've seen and experienced Universal Oneness, and I know that It is in every one of us. Its gift is what It is: creative energy, pure potential, pure unadulterated possibility. It doesn't choose for us, It cannot. It simply says, "Yes." We have an opportunity to reveal our undesirable beliefs that the Universe is saying "Yes" to and replace them with new beliefs that we would like to experience the Universe saying "Yes" to. I know it's simple, though not always easy ... but what else are you going to do? *When do you think will be a better time to change your belief systems and experience the life you were meant to live?* The best time is now.

Never underestimate the power of repetition; it is the most effective way to change your beliefs and radically change your experience. You can't align your thinking with positive and enlightening ideas without a conscious decision to expose yourself to those ideas repeatedly. The world around you can be very negative, fearful, and steeped in limited ideas. The media is louder and more influential than it has ever been.

Let's face it; unless one consciously chooses to *repetitively* imprint oneself with positive ideas, and *repetitively* aligns one's mind with the Universal Wisdom that is available, he or she simply ends up living in fear, doubt, and limitation. That does not have to be *your* reality! That does not have to be *your* life! You can set yourself free.

Repetition is not just about repeating affirmations until you're blue in the face; it's about consistently aligning with Divine Intelligence and repeatedly engaging in the awakening process. This Divine Intelligence, as part of who you are, is calling you to awaken to It. In order to experience this aligning, you must break the spell of the illusions created by your own limiting belief systems. These beliefs have held you captive in the recesses of your limited imagination, but it doesn't have to be this way.

Repetition is the key to this awakening process. You can't lose when you consistently apply the principles of repetition. A rewarding life awaits you. Why not give it a try?

> **KEY**
>
> *The only thing that limits us is ourselves, our belief systems, and our perceptions. Change them and our lives change: it's that simple.*

Sleep your way to greater success

One of the easiest and most effective tools I have discovered is the practice of sleep-repetition learning, in which you listen to soothing, positive ideas while you sleep. Sleep-repetition is one way to offset a myriad of negative influences in your world by utilizing your downtime to positively imprint the subconscious mind with supportive, life-affirming, unifying beliefs, in an easy and effortless way.

One third of your life is spent sleeping. Now you can reclaim that lost time! Sleep-repetition learning is fast, easy, and effective, and is just one of the powerful transformational tools in this book. Virtually every authority in the personal growth movement recognizes the immense importance of repetition. *This is the first book that makes that most important practice its focus.*

The practice of positive sleep-repetition speeds up your exposure to positive information. When your conscious mind is asleep, it doesn't argue with the positive input; your subconscious mind simply receives the eight hours of continuous, uninterrupted, life-affirming information. This input offsets the negativity that is unconsciously received and the negativity that *is* consciously chosen during the day.

You will begin to notice an increased sense of well-being, hopefulness, and positivity as the supportive beliefs become established and are reinforced by your daily practices of spiritual growth. Repetition is the KEY, and as you establish a repetitive practice, every night, you will see and feel the difference. Later in this book I will further discuss the benefits of sleep-repetition learning.

Children exposed to positive programming through sleep-repetition have remarkable results because they are not reprogramming negative beliefs as much as they are reinforcing positive beliefs that are naturally inherent in all children. This strong foundation will continue to attract circumstances that mirror their early beliefs.

> The first sleep-repetition learning recording that I ever made for my children included a lullaby that I sang. They listened to it over and over again …
>
> *You are special, you're unique, you're the one that*
> *I love.*
> *Listen now, to the words, I am speaking of.*
> *You're the one, like the sun, brightens up my life,*
> *Oh my darling, I love you.*
> *Listen to the words that I speak,*
> *As I tell of light and love.*
> *You are the one that's special to me,*
> *You're the one I'm dreaming of.*
> *You are special, you're unique, you're the one that*
> *I love,*
> *Listen now, to the words, I am speaking of.*
> *Yes it's true, it is you, you're the one that I love,*

> *Oh my darling, I love you, oh my darling, I love you.*
>
> I followed with words of affirmation to tell them how they were loved, creative, intelligent, and so forth. I played this message for my two little girls over and over again, using an auto-reverse cassette player so they would hear it all night. They slept peacefully and contentedly. They wouldn't go to bed without it and to this day, all of my kids still listen to positive and supportive messages and music while they sleep.
>
> When my third child Peter was born, life was unbearably difficult. My husband had been out of consistent work for nearly two years, we had no money, and the dark, gloomy house we lived in was difficult to tolerate. From the moment I brought Peter home from the hospital, I declared his life would be very different from our current situation. I began to play tapes on developing the millionaire mindset for him all night and day while he slept. (See page ?? to learn how this impacted Peter as he grew.)

I will show you how positive repetition practices can radically transform your life and how you can make positive repetition a permanent lifestyle practice, not just a fad diet. These practices and the insight that they bring can change your life.

Stay open; keep in mind that you are experiencing life through the lens of your belief systems, and if you don't like what you see, you can change your beliefs. This book will show you how a few changes in the way you view life can change everything.

Simplify and discover your power

Transformation of all kinds happens as a result of committing ourselves to positive change. Right now, if you are reading these words, I know your soul is calling for a transformation. Something in you knows that life should be better than it is for you at present. Something in you knows that you really were created for joy and abundance. Something in you is calling you home, home to greater peace and awakening.

My heart cries out to you; I want to wrap my arms around you, encourage you, and tell you that your soul's desire for greater expression, life, and abundance can be your destiny. There is something within you that is screaming to be recognized, loved, and honored. You must listen to this voice, honor its wisdom, and allow it to guide you home to greater joy, lasting peace, and happiness. This book will give you the tools to reconnect to this center and find peace in its presence.

You may have been trained to not listen to this inner voice of wisdom. It may have been blocked by the myriad of belief systems that you have been conditioned to accept. One way these belief systems show up is in the inner voice of the critic, saying things like, "I'm not good enough. What will people think?" or "I should've done it better." This book will help you recognize and begin to starve the voice of the doubting critic and begin to feed the voice of love and empowerment. **Repetition is the key.**

There is an ancient story about a young Indian boy that went to his wise grandfather and said, "Grandfather, I feel like I have two wild dogs fighting inside of me. One is trying to get away and the other one keeps pulling me back into the fight. Which one will win?"

And the grandfather wisely replied, "The one that you feed."

That message, so simply and powerfully put, is the essence of this book on the power of repetition. Do not let the simplicity of this message fool you into thinking that it is not powerful. Learning to simply and repetitively take responsibility for your life, your thoughts, and your beliefs is the difference between an evolved and empowered person and one who continues to suffer in fear, pain, and limitation. The question I ask you now and invite you to think about often, is, "Which thoughts will *you* feed?"

This story is my story. What I've learned, you can learn, too. I know that the processes and systems I teach can transform your life for good, and I know that sleep-repetition learning is an easy practice anyone can use. Isn't it time to move forward in life and win the battle over the small, limiting voices of the past? Turn the page and give yourself permission to live the life you want to live!

> *We are what we think. All that we are arises with our thoughts. With our thoughts we make our world. –Buddha*

CHAPTER TWO

BUILD A STRONG FOUNDATION

As a child, I remember hearing the story of the "Three Little Pigs." I'm sure you remember it, too, but let me paraphrase it briefly in my own grown-up words. There are three little pigs that grow up and, finding it is time to start their lives as grown-up pigs, decide to build their own individual homes.

The first little pig is in a hurry; he wants to go play. So he quickly gathers some straw, shabbily builds his house, and off to play he goes.

The second little pig is a bit more diligent; he gathers some sticks and puts them together as best he can to build his house. He is glad it is done and goes out to play.

The third little pig is much more thorough; he wants a house that is sturdy and strong. He takes lots of time to discover how to build a house; he gets the supplies, tools, and the professional help he needs; and although it takes a long time, he eventually builds a strong house out of bricks and mortar. Then, he goes out to play.

Well, wouldn't you know it, eventually the big bad wolf comes into the story. He goes up to the first little piggy who built his house out of straw, knocks on the door, and growls at the pig, "Little pig, little pig, let me come in!"

And the little pig yells, "No, not by the hair of my chinny-chin-chin!"

The wolf growls back, "Then I'll huff and I'll puff and I'll blow your house down!" And, of course, he huffs and puffs and, very easily, blows the house down.

Well, as you know, the wolf then goes on to the next little pig and repeats the whole episode: he huffs and he puffs and he blows the whole stick house down.

The third little pig, however, is calm, collected, and unconcerned by the wolf's antics as he tries to intimidate him. As before, the wolf huffs and puffs, but we all know that a little hot air won't blow down a house built out of brick and mortar.

Eliminate weak beliefs and build strong ones

Like the three grown-up pigs in our story above, we all get to that point as adults when we are responsible for our own lives. We can no longer rely on our parents or anyone else; we must build our own houses. Sometimes we're simply in a hurry and don't want to take the time to carefully assess what it takes to build our lives on a strong foundation; but as the hasty piggies discover in our story, being hasty does not pay in the long run.

If we take the time to examine our beliefs, we can determine which beliefs serve us and which do not. Which beliefs will be there to support us when the wolves come knocking at our door? Will we believe that we are helpless little creatures, that life is hard, that the world is scary? Or will we believe that everything we need is provided, that we have the necessary strength, and that we will allow the Infinite Wisdom to guide and protect us?

The choice is always up to us. We can make a conscious decision to build our house of beliefs with a strong foundation.

> *Therefore everyone who hears these words of mine and puts them into practice is like a wise man who built his house on the rock. The rain came down, the streams rose, and the winds blew and beat against that house; yet it did not fall, because it had its foundation on the rock.*
> —**Matthew 7:24-25**

Your belief system is your foundation. Is it built on the rock? Ernest Holmes, an early twentieth-century philosopher wrote, "THE WHOLE teaching of Jesus was based on the theory that we are surrounded by an intelligent Law, which does unto each as he believes. He implied the necessity of faith, conviction, and acceptance."

That is, blessings must be measured out to us according to our own measuring. We must not only believe, we must know that our belief measures the extent and degree of our blessing. If our belief is limited, only a little can come to us, because that is as we believe. We call this the law of mental equivalents. How much life can *you* experience? As much as *you* can embody.

Overcome your early programming

The belief systems that were mirrored for us as children are automatically accepted until we reach the age of reason and begin to pick and choose new belief systems. These beliefs are patterns that affect the way we view life. We can begin to change these belief systems by making a *conscious choice* to change them. These patterns are usually very strong, so it must be a choice that takes place more than once.

I, like you, have seen many people overcome their early childhood programming to become so much more—and that is what I know is possible for all of us, when we consciously choose. We are building our new foundation now, and it doesn't matter how old we are, or how long we have believed that we are separate, alone, or limited. Today is a new day, and our beliefs can be changed when we apply the principles of repetition!

Everyone reading this has accepted many new belief systems. For example, most of us, if we're over twenty-five, were not raised on computers; we didn't have a belief system in place that said we can go to a box on the table, punch in words and numbers, and visit places all over the world with endless information right at our fingertips. We now believe that we can because we've seen and done it. We have also seen abused children grow up to overcome their early programming and make something of themselves. We've seen impoverished kids grow up to become very successful. We have seen many people grow beyond their limited beginnings.

You, too, have grown up believing that you were limited in some way, and you have overridden that belief system by proving it wrong. You made a decision to see life differently: you have chosen new beliefs in many areas of your life, and you have experienced the benefits those choices brought to you. But I know you, like me, have experienced the results of painful, divisive belief systems, creating experiences that are less than satisfying, belief systems that have sabotaged your efforts at greater joy, satisfaction, love, and success. In order to have a new experience in life, we must learn to accept new, more positive, supportive, life-affirming belief systems over and over again. We are adults now, and we are not destined to repeat and live out those previously accepted belief systems.

> *We may change the trend of causation, which has been set in motion, at any time we decide to do so.*
> —**Ernest Holmes**

Understand how old beliefs operate and new ones form

Recognizing the beliefs that no longer serve you is the first step in choosing new beliefs. Imagine that your subconscious mind is like a large and complex filing system and storehouse. It stores everything you've ever thought, said, or seen. Imagine that every idea you are exposed to gets filed in this complex system of filing cabinets and folders. Some folders are very thick and some are not. The really thick folders represent the beliefs you have established and reinforced over the years; these beliefs have a way of influencing your perception and how you view life.

This huge filing system not only stores information but is also powerfully creative. Like a software program, it has the ability to create circumstances for you when you access the file folders that you have created. The program naturally draws from those file folders that are filled with all your thoughts and feelings. Now, this creative storehouse isn't going to choose for you; it cannot. It simply receives all the information you have gathered and follows the instructions that you give it. The thick folders tend to draw you toward, focus you on, circumstances that match your current belief system—unless you start to reverse the pattern.

> I grew up in a large family with seven children. My father was a positive man, who instilled in me the power of hope. But, more often than not, promises were not kept. I heard, "We're going to do this," or "We're going to get you that." When it didn't happen, it left me with the belief that my dreams couldn't come true.
>
> I was the daughter of a dreamer and I learned to dream, too. But I also learned to sabotage myself before those dreams could come true. Many experiences of almost getting what I wanted began to show up in my life. As I learned new principles, I began to recognize

> old patterns of belief at work, and I chose to consciously create new patterns to replace them.

Many times when we are experiencing pain in our lives, we have been called to the storehouse to see what it is we believe. If we are willing to look at the folder responsible for attracting certain undesirable circumstances and then attempt to heal and let go of beliefs by consciously creating new folders and filling them with repetitive practices, we can begin to experience the lasting transformation we desire. If we are unwilling to look at the problem file folders, we will continue to create the unwanted circumstances. It's always our choice.

> I remember when I bought my first new car, a small red Hyundai. It was a big deal for me; I was a single mother, had three kids, and was just starting to see over the pile of bills. Two days later, the car was stolen from in front of my apartment. I felt immediately as I had felt when I was a child—I had almost gotten what I wanted.
>
> That very day I decided I could change this belief system, and I immediately began to affirm that it was okay to have what I wanted and I could have it now. I repeatedly affirmed that it was okay for me to accept this good, and good could come to me. After a few days of affirming these things, my car was returned to me.
>
> Years later, I got another car. After two weeks of having that car, it was stolen from my driveway. Again, I recognized the same pain of disappointment. I began to affirm over and over again, "It's okay for me to have what I want. I can keep my cars. I deserve the best, I deserve a nice car, and I will accept the car of my dreams."

> Well, this time my car was not found, but I got the insurance money and bought the car I really wanted, a bright red convertible! Even after I had that shiny red car in my possession, I continued to tell myself over and over that it was wonderful for me to have this dream car and I could keep it. Keep it I did; in fact, I wore it out!

Another important aspect of this storage room of beliefs is that it is also connected to everyone else's storage room. There's actually just one big storage room, and we all have our file folders in it. It's called collective mind, or collective consciousness. Others' beliefs can and do affect you; that is why it is so important to consciously choose the people you associate with—their beliefs eventually become your beliefs. Your evolved belief systems lift up the collective community as well. In other words, as you continue to repetitively choose new thoughts, beliefs, and perceptions, others are blessed and lifted up with you.

Choose new thoughts and positive affirmations to create new life experiences. Remember that your conscious choice is the director of this storage room. In other words, through conscious choice you pack the file folders with the beliefs that create your life. If you do not use your conscious choice repetitively to choose new beliefs, you will unconsciously substantiate and continue to pack the files full of negative, limiting beliefs. Obviously, if you have stacks and stacks of folders that say, "I am poor and limited," a few positive affirmations of "I am abundant in every way" are not going to be that effective.

In fact, when you try to input a new positive idea into the storage room, the conscious mind usually argues with it. For example, what happens to you when I say, "You are a millionaire"?

The first thing your mind may say back to you is, "I am not."

The positive input, either from yourself or someone external to you, is completely nullified by your arguing conscious mind. You added one file for the abundance and one for the limitation: it's a wash.

You need to have more positive input than negative. ***That is why sleep-repetition learning is so powerful.*** When your conscious mind is asleep, or unaware, it is not arguing for your limitation or against the positive input you are being exposed to. It is especially effective when you repeatedly tell yourself to listen to the commands you are receiving, such as, "I want to hear these positive suggestions and I intend to reprogram my old beliefs." When you do this your storage and creative facility begins immediately to act on these commands.

> *Here is a most significant fact—the subconscious mind takes any orders given it in a spirit of absolute faith and acts upon those orders, although the orders have to be repeated over and over again, through repetition, before they are interpreted by the subconscious mind.*
>
> *—Napoleon Hill,*
> ***Author of Think and Grow Rich***

Repetition will produce re-cognition. Changing belief systems requires one to use his or her will, the power of choice, and repetitive programming practices. Repetition produces a re-cognition of internal reality. Changing beliefs requires being conscious of when you're thinking in the same old way or regurgitating the same old ideas, beginning to choose again.

In addition to engaging in repetitive learning practices, you will want to associate with others who accept the beliefs you are trying to accept.

Remember, their beliefs influence you—you share the same storage facility; we are all connected. When you change the contents of your storage and creative facility, you also help everyone else.

> I once worked in an investment firm in Los Angeles. It was a speculative company and we were promised quite a bit—great perks, more money, new offices, etc. At one point, we kept being promised we would be paid "on Friday." This went on for five weeks without pay. I was a single mother who lived paycheck to paycheck, and how we survived this one was truly a miracle.
>
> Finally, I became aware that working without pay was a familiar pattern. I began to affirm, "I surrender this old pattern; it no longer serves me. I give it up, I let it go! I deserve to get paid for my work. I accept payment for my time at work. I deserve all that I am promised. God is my source; I depend upon no outside channel for my good."
>
> I finally stood my ground and left the company. I was clear that I would not work for people who would promise and not deliver. I would have to say "no" to what I didn't want in order to say "yes" to what I did want! I left that job with no other job in sight. Within a couple of days I got a call from someone who found out that I had left my job, asking me to come to their company.
>
> By the way, I got paid more money, and payday happened every Friday!

When challenges and pain come our way, we can simply ask if there is a belief system in place that no longer serves us; if this is the case, we can begin to affirm a new belief system. **This process of affirming new beliefs**

must become a pattern for life. If we do this only once in a while, we will see little result. We can learn to challenge the beliefs that we have automatically accepted, rather than just blame ourselves or someone else for what happened. I could have easily blamed the thief who stole my car or the employer who didn't deliver, but that would not have served me. I simply began the work of creating a new belief system.

> **KEY**
>
> *Taking responsibility for our life experiences and emotions does not mean blaming and shaming ourselves. That is like putting new wine in old wineskins, and taking new teachings and using them in an old way. Taking responsibility for your life is the fastest way I know to grow.*

I have learned, over and over again, that if we are willing to keep our eyes open and learn from our life's experiences, we can grow out of the old patterns and transform our lives. My life today is so very different than it used to be twenty, ten, and even five years ago. It has progressively become better, because I have consciously chosen to look at my beliefs and repetitively choose new ones. I look at many of the people I knew years ago, even some of those in my own family, and their lives are not much different now than they were twenty years ago: it's the same old, same old, and that breaks my heart. We have so much power to recreate our lives, but the problem I see most frequently is the lack of willingness to take responsibility for our beliefs. We must evaluate our beliefs honestly and then be conscious and repetitive about creating new ones.

> *Begin to blot out, one by one, all false beliefs—all ideas that man is limited, poor, or miserable. Refuse to think of failure or to doubt your own power. See only what you wish to experience and look at nothing else ... We are not depending on a reed shaken by the wind, but on the Principle of Life Itself, for all that we have or ever shall need. It is not some power, or a great power, it is ALL POWER. Our belief sets the limit to our demonstration of a Principle, which of Itself, is without limit.*
>
> —*Ernest Holmes*

Claim your spiritual freedom

Our early religious beliefs are some of the most potent and powerful beliefs that shape our destiny. They can serve us, or not. God is a very big idea. Many people were raised with the notion of a very loving God who was, however, prone to temper tantrums.

I grew up believing that God loves me when I'm good and withdraws from me when I'm bad. Ask a hundred different people to describe their childhood beliefs about God, heaven, and hell, and you will get similar responses. There is fear and love, all mixed up together. Do it right, you're loved; do it wrong, you could burn forever.

Our beliefs about God are paramount to our experiences in life. They can color our perceptions, create prejudices, and also establish positive values. They can be very difficult to change, and if they are supportive, they can assist us in building a strong spiritual foundation, carrying us throughout life's struggles and changes. However, if they are confusing and damaging, those beliefs can haunt us for life, making the voices of the past ring in our ears for years to come—believe me, I know.

I was raised in a multi-generational family in which members from both sides followed the same religion. We called it *the* church. Everything was about *the* church. Our very identity was based upon our place in *the* church. It was *the only* true church, and, growing up in this teaching, we unconsciously accepted that others who were not part of *the* church were not quite as acceptable.

No one in the family ever left *the* church—that is, until my mother did. Of course, she was called a heretic, a satanic, and every other derogatory name you could imagine. But she was the only woman I had ever known that lived a nearly saintly life! She was a deeply spiritual woman with an open mind (God forbid!). She found God everywhere. However, she was treated like a leper by her own family.

> I was nineteen years old when my mom's brother came to visit. My parents were separating and I was living for a short time with my father and my three younger sisters. It was a time of great pain as we watched our parents go through the dissolution of their twenty-five-year marriage. My mother was leaving the church as well. It was unthinkable, blasphemous, and an abomination to her family. Not to me, of course. I was nineteen years old and I was sick of the church anyway.
>
> My parents could not go through this shameful experience in their hometown; instead, they moved to California, as a happy family, in order to then separate and have no one know. It was my mother who wanted to leave. She knew of no other way to get out of her unhappiness but to say, "God told me to leave; leave the church, leave the family, and follow Him."
>
> We sat in the living room of our new California home: my

father, three sisters, my uncle, and me. My uncle had traveled a great distance to let my sisters and me know that our mother had fallen into the hands of Satan. She was now under the control of Satan and we should not listen to her or see her. He went on and on as my father nodded and listened. It was much easier to blame Satan than to actually look at personal issues in their marriage, I suppose.

I'll never forget though, as soon as my sisters and I could get ourselves away from them, we gathered together in the closet. We knew they were wrong because we knew our mother and saw through their fears. We sat huddled in a circle away from the ears or eyes of our uncle and we prayed. We knew that our mother was okay and we prayed that she would be safe. In that secret and precious moment, we vowed that no matter what direction our lives would take us, we would always love each other unconditionally. We promised that we would never abandon one another because of which church we attended. We agreed there had been enough wars over religion in this world.

My mother, through her own example and sacrifices, gave me permission to seek for myself—to keep an open mind and follow my heart. By her refusal to believe in only one path, she encouraged me to trust the voice of my own insight and encouraged me to believe that there might just be more than one way to heaven. She gave me permission to think that there is no greater joy than to feel the experience of God, in my own personal and private way. Thank God for her wisdom. I would rely heavily upon her example in the days ahead when my own spiritual crisis arrived in full force.

It was nearly the last straw; I'd had all I could take with this church. I gathered my three children, ages two, five, and eight, into the car with my husband grumbling and complaining; we had survived another long and grueling Sunday morning. It was the last time I ever wanted to hear the church leader tell us how we were the chosen people, the righteous ones, and the only rightful inheritors of the kingdom of heaven. The one and only true church. I had heard it one too many times.

Then there was the continued guidance by the church leaders to support and follow my husband's lead; because he was the one "God chose" to be the leader of our family. While that might be fine for some, I felt and knew in my heart that his leadership was leading us into poverty, chaos, and misery. I prayed, I read, I craved a new spirituality. My ultimate release was experienced when I finally decided if the members of my church were the only ones going to heaven, I did not want to go there with them. At that moment I mentally began to set myself free.

One day soon after, I "accidentally" walked into a church called the Positive Living Center, in Fresno, California. The warmth and friendliness of the minister, Reverend Tom Sannar, was utterly refreshing and unlike anything I had experienced. I looked around their bookstore and saw familiar books, some of which I had read and hidden underneath my bed. Little did I know how that day would change the shape of my life. There was only one problem. Their church service was at the same time as mine. I would have to choose. And it really scared me to have to choose.

I felt like I was in between two worlds. I wanted desperately to get out of one and into another one, but I was utterly terrified. I was afraid of what my husband would do; I was afraid of what

> my family would say; I was afraid of what my husband's family would say; and I was afraid of what people would think of me. I was most afraid for my children. What if I was wrong?

Just because someone gives you permission to believe something new or explore new ideas, doesn't mean that the old beliefs aren't like sticky tar on a hot day. For years, I fought with the voices of the elderly white men in my mind (God and spiritual authority images to me). I battled with the new ideas that I was studying.

I was loving and drinking in this new knowledge that was telling me I was just as worthy as anyone else and just as able to live at my highest level. I was savoring all the tasty tidbits of truth, knowledge of Universal Laws, and principles that govern life. I was discovering God as a Universal Love and Power that was always available and operating all the time through me. I was learning that there was nothing that could separate me from God but my own thoughts and beliefs. I was learning about how my thoughts and beliefs were creating my reality, and that if I could change my beliefs I could change my life. That news excited and thrilled me.

I was given tools that would put me in the driver's seat instead of the back seat, where I had sat previously—always hoping that someone, anyone, would take me where I wanted to go. I discovered that when you learn these principles and begin to take responsibility for your beliefs and recreate them through repetitive practices, then you're in the driver's seat choosing where you want to go. Beware of something else happening: there may be voices in the back seat or the back recesses of your mind, arguing with your new-found freedom. These voices are the voices of the past and nothing more—they do not drive the car unless you turn it over to them. The repetitive practices of affirming the new truth and thinking new thoughts can prevail.

> *What would it feel like to have a totally guilt-free life? I would go to the church of my choice, I would seek God freely in my own heart. I would be very spiritual because guilt would no longer separate me from God. I would teach my children freely about Universal Laws and encourage their growth and experience. I would not worry or be concerned about what others thought of me and how I lived my life.*
>
> As I read these lines over in my journal, I knew that my soul screamed to be released from the self-imposed guilt and belief systems that kept me trapped in a world of pain and suffering. I willed myself to push through my fears and choose my own life, imperfect or not. I chose the new world.
>
> I began attending the church that would become my new home. I ate up the knowledge, took classes, attended workshops, and studied. Although the old voices of the past continued for years, the thirst for more and more of this new knowledge prevailed.

Take a stand for *your* spiritual beliefs: it is the most important thing you can do for yourself. This is the one area that is yours. It is your most precious right. I know it is frightening—I have been rejected, and I have been ridiculed. I know it's scary to break away from conditioned rules and structures, but it was the one thing that I would not—could not—allow any other person to do for me. My spiritual path is mine; it's intimate and not to be chosen by anyone but me. Deep in the recesses of my soul is my path, and, granted, it may be different from yours. I urge you to grant yourself the freedom to choose your own path, today and always.

> "Where is Janette?" they would ask my now ex-husband at church.
>
> I'm not sure how he responded. Eventually, the leader of my old church called me in to talk to him. When I told him I would not be attending anymore and that I had decided to go to another church, I had to endure the next level of guilt.
>
> "What about your children? Their eternal salvation is at stake. I hope you have the decency to think about them before you do something that could separate them forever from God."

> *When we know our Oneness with God and Law, a great burden is removed. Any sense of opposition is removed from the consciousness which perceives Unity. If we think of ourselves as being separated from the Universe, we shall be limited by this thought, for it is the belief in separation from God which binds and limits. WE ARE BOUND BY NOTHING EXCEPT BELIEF. They could not enter in because of their unbelief, and because they limited the Holy One of Israel.*
>
> —*Ernest Holmes*

Know with whom and what you identify

In our lives we identify with many different people, experiences, and identities. My daughter Arielle was a creative, artistic, dramatic child. She changed her identity quite a bit. We would joke, "Who are you today?"

"I am Ariel, the mermaid!" she would say, or perhaps, "Today I am the Queen of Sheba," or whoever was on TV at the time. As she grew older, I noticed she would become like the friends she would associate with, or the boyfriends she chose. She changed in form and identity more dramatically than some of us, but we all do this—I do it, you do it.

We become like that upon which we focus our attention. It's Metaphysics 101. ***Where your attention goes, your energy flows.*** The people and beliefs that we identify with establish the patterns that create our lives. If we do nothing but engage in violent movies, books, or music, we will experience violence in us—perhaps not as extreme as that which we watch, but it is no less influential.

If we spend a lot of time in spiritual pursuits, seeking to know the nature of the Divine experience, we will begin to experience ourselves having the same qualities that we contemplate. If we seek to learn about successful people in business or any field whatsoever, we will begin to identify with them, learn from them, and become like them. This is a scientific truth of human nature that must be taken into account.

Most of us can accept this truth, but we forget the degree to which it is always working. How can we prosper if we never have before, and if we don't now expose ourselves *regularly* to prosperous ideas, people, or places? If our belief systems have been based in financial limitation—that is, we've learned to think in terms of limitation or our experiences in life have been in limitation—we can expect to continue to live in limitation.

If we don't want a life of limitation, we need to know that these beliefs were not created overnight and they may not change overnight. We must *repetitively* begin to think differently. We must choose some new friends and begin to study happy and successful people—begin to emulate them, and identify with them. Identifying ourselves in a new way is key to living a new reality and creating lasting transformation.

> For many years I identified myself as a struggling single mother. I clung to this all of the time. I was proud of myself for being so strong and handling so much. "Wow!" people would say, "You are so strong, I just don't know how you do it." And I would mutter something humble.
>
> Eventually I began to see how I was getting rewarded for struggling. I was unconsciously choosing to struggle, choosing to live a hard life, choosing to get attention for my strength. *Well, if I can create struggle*, I thought, *couldn't I create happiness and ease?*
>
> That insight began the practice of creating a new belief system that said, "Life is good. I am provided for easily and effortlessly. I don't have to struggle. God didn't create me to struggle, but to live life in joy and abundance. My good comes to me easily and effortlessly. I change my thinking and I change my life. I am completely supported and sustained. Life is easy. All I need comes to me."
>
> From then on, every time I saw struggle I knew that I could choose an easier way. This eventually began to change my surroundings, my support, and my level of life. Life is not a struggle for me now; life is joyful. All that I need comes easily and effortlessly, and the path is made straight before me. Why not?

With whom and what do you identify? I believe that the greatest idea we can affirm, discover, and know is that we can all identify with God or whatever name we might call this Higher Power.

God is love, and so are you. God is Light, and so are you. God is Peace, and so are you. God is Power, and so are you. God is Joy, and so are you. God is Beauty, and so are you.

You are a divine spark of the Godhead. You may have forgotten—most of us do. We begin to forget the day we are born. We begin to identify as human beings in flesh and bone, and learn from our parents what that means. We forget that we are spiritual beings. The more we seek to identify with that which we truly are—spiritual beings, whole and complete—the more we begin to experience the effects of that belief. You are Spirit and so am I. Let's remember together.

> *Today I identify myself as a joyful spiritual being, completely supported, sustained, and supplied.*

CHAPTER THREE

IDENTIFY AND ABOLISH LIMITING BELIEFS

Assess and identify your personal beliefs

Learning to live from the awareness that your internal world creates your external world is a powerful step in your own personal evolution, growth, and expansion. **It is the most powerful knowledge you can discover.** It is like finding Aladdin's lamp when you begin to realize that your destiny is in your own hands. Accepting this knowledge as truth and living it consciously are two different things! Why? Because you are a creature of habit, and the habits you have can be strong deterrents to your own happiness and success. That is why knowing that you are a creative being is not enough.

    A great many people know their thoughts and beliefs create their reality, and yet they feel utterly helpless in their efforts at transformation. I believe that your own transformation is the greatest work you can do! And you will find that engaging in the activity of transforming the old limited beliefs that were handed down to you, generation after generation, can and does make a difference, not only in your own life, but in the lives of your children and the generations to come.

This conscious transformation also adds to the collective awareness and evolution of ideas that continue to create the world that others will inhabit. Your personal efforts at transformation change the world! You may worry about the world and the problems you see around you, but know this: **The best thing you can do for the world is heal yourself.** Until you get strong, whole, and free, you're absolutely ineffective in creating powerful positive change in the world!

You have a set of beliefs that determines your viewpoint, perceptions, and experiences in life. You may work externally to change your life's experiences, but unless you do the inner work necessary, the changes do not stick.

Imagine that you set your thermostat in your house for 72°. It will maintain that temperature. Now, you can leave a door open and if it is hotter outside the outside air will heat up the house, but the thermostat will continue to cool down the house until it comes back to 72°. If it is winter and the door is left open, the house will get cold, but the thermostat will do its job and bring the temperature back up to 72°. No matter what you do externally, the thermostat tells the heating or cooling system what to do in order to bring the temperature of the room back to where you have it set.

Now, you must understand that you, too, have internal thermostats. Let's imagine that you have an internal thermostat that says that money is hard to come by, there's never enough money to go around, or that it's not spiritual to have money. If your internal thermostat is set with certain limitations, no matter what you do to create opportunities for more money in your life, it will bring you back to what you internally believe. Can't you see how important it is to work on the internal programming that creates lasting change? **It is the most important work you can do.**

How do you know what your internal programming is? **Look at your life.** Imagine if you had an apple tree in the backyard that was loaded with delicious, juicy apples. You would be pretty sure the roots that produced that fruit were roots of an apple tree, wouldn't you? Now, look at the fruits of your life, and you will begin to get some clues about what your "root" beliefs are.

Solve your problems at the level of the roots or the cause, not at the level of the fruits or the effects! Until you learn to think this way and live this way, you will never have any lasting transformation.

When you understand and see how your outer world is created by your inner world, you will get to work on your inner world, every day, every week, every month, every year! The repetitively chosen thoughts you have today are creating your tomorrows. The reactions you have today are simply showing you what you believe.

Once you know what limiting beliefs you hold, it's time to begin to choose anew. Moment by moment you are choosing what to believe, whether you are aware of it or not. Everyone is creating their lives, but most do it unconsciously. *Transformation begins to occur when you get conscious of this process.* Begin to identify what your beliefs are; question them and choose again. And by the way, do it again and again.

You are more than what you see. You are a being that is physical, mental, emotional, and spiritual. The physical you and the world around you could be likened to a tree's fruits. They are what you see. But the other parts of you, that which you don't see, could be likened to a tree's roots. The roots create the fruits. In order for you to have different fruits on your tree, it is the roots that must change. Blaming the fruits does not change the roots!

Question your limited beliefs, gain understanding

I met a man and thought he was a nice guy. He was fun to be with and we had a good time. He was dependable and did everything he said he'd do. He was stable, reliable, kind, supportive, and an all-around good human being. He wanted the same things I did, and we shared the same values. But, I wasn't all that interested in him. He didn't match my internal programming.

My head said, *He's a good man and fits what I've wanted to attract.* Yet, my emotional programming wasn't stimulating the passion dance that was usually reserved for the relationships that could never work. **My internal thermostat was still set for unavailable men, big promisers, and little producers.** I still craved the wild ride rather than the stable and secure relationship that would bring me what I truly wanted to experience. Fortunately by this time in my life, I was willing to continue to work on my internal programming before throwing away a perfectly good man! Actually, I did try to throw him away; fortunately for both of us, he didn't give up on me and, more importantly, I didn't give up on me.

"I'm not ready for commitment," I said to Mike. I wanted to date other men. I wasn't sure if he was the one for me and I didn't want to get tied down. That didn't work for Mike. If I wasn't ready for commitment then he didn't need me. He was a one-woman man and he wanted a woman that would play at that level. I was afraid. We broke it off.

This began a time of soul searching for me. For years I had been saying I wanted commitment, intimacy, and marriage. And then when there was someone who was telling me that was what he wanted, I was running. I told myself that I wasn't and could never be in love with him. I didn't recognize that a negative belief pattern was creating my perceptions, so I simply made excuses.

After a couple of months of loneliness and sadness, I began to crack the interior shell of the beliefs that would keep me alone. I finally surrendered deeply to Infinite Wisdom which knew better than my old programming. "Help me see this differently," I prayed. "I don't know how to do relationships. Please help me do it differently. I choose a loving, committed relationship and I trust in Universal Wisdom to help me be the person who can experience it."

I continued to affirm, to pray, and to write. I allowed myself to dream of marriage, commitment, and surrendering to a new choice of what I wanted in life. I affirmed over and over that I was lovable, I was worthy, and I deserved to share my life with a partner. I would accept a worthy partner into my life. I affirmed over and over, "I am love and I am lovable. I am worthy of love. I can be nothing but love. It is who I am. I choose now to live life in a partnership and I attract the right person who shares this desire." I didn't want to continue this pattern of loneliness in my life. I knew I wanted life in partnership rather than life alone, and I wanted a worthy partner. I finally began to shift the pattern of belief in me to one that could accept this kind of man into my life.

Then something happened that I can't explain. I began to see Mike differently. Something in me had shifted; my vision and my perception changed. He was a different man. I fell in love with him. And the rest is history. We got back together and married a year later. We celebrated our fifth wedding anniversary this year.

Being in partnership is another way to do life; I like and choose it now. You, too, can cultivate conscious, deliberate choice. You are the chooser. And, you get to choose again and again. Relationships can be so much more joyful when you realize that your experiences are not so much about the other person as they are about you. Relationships can reveal your beliefs. They reveal the places in you where you have believed in your unworthiness, your separateness, and your insecurities.

Change your beliefs, change your life. In order to experience living with greater success, love, and peace, you must have a change of beliefs at a deep subconscious level or you will keep repeating the same old programs.

Unravel the seven core beliefs that undermine your success

The following ideas represent beliefs (or variations of beliefs) that most people hold at some level. These ideas undermine your potential and block you from living the life of your dreams. They continually reinforce the idea that you are a victim and that someone else or some external experience is responsible for your joy, happiness, and success.

Look at your life to see where you feel victimized—whether it's real or imagined—and begin to look for the underlying beliefs that are operating. Then, begin to reprogram these beliefs **consistently and repetitively** by affirming new beliefs so that the old beliefs are less and less operative as the roots that are growing your fruits!

Seven Undermining Beliefs
1. I am not worthy

This belief is like a disease in a lot of people. There may have been continual messages given to you as a child that required certain conditions for you to feel worthy.

> *What do you need to do to feel worthy?*
> *Does it work and is it ever enough?*

The truth is that you are worthy because you exist! Your right to life, love, and happiness were given to you by the Creator of *all* life, and you are a part of life and are worthy to have it all, be it all, and express it all. You can't see that as long as you hold on to the belief that you are unworthy.

How to recognize when this unhealthy belief is triggered:

An event occurs in your life that makes you feel bad, sad, disappointed, fearful, or angered. Some good is not forthcoming. When you ask yourself the question, *What is it that I am telling myself?* the thought may come up, *I don't feel that I am worthy.* When that happens, you must take the energy of the pain and transmute it in a way that causes a shift to take place. Remember, you must allow yourself to feel the emotion. This triggers that unsupportive belief operating in you.

You release the belief by observing it, not by denying it. Remember, your perception of any experience is colored by your beliefs. You reprogram your perception! You don't have to perceive your experience from a viewpoint determined by a belief in your unworthiness. Everything that happens is just an experience. It is your belief that gives it meaning.

> *Nothing has meaning except the meaning you give it.*

Affirm with energy:

> ***Just because something doesn't happen in the way I wanted does not mean that I am unworthy. I am worthy—no matter what happens in my life. I am worthy simply because I am alive. I don't need outer circumstances to change for me to feel worthy. I am worthwhile and my life matters. The universe loves and supports me, and I am worthy of the best. I am worthy because I AM. I am enough. I am worthy.***

2. There is not enough

Whether it's money, time, love, friends, happiness, or whatever, there is a belief that there is not enough to make you happy, loved, or satisfied. The real problem is that there is a belief that something outside of yourself is lacking. Maybe your tree has produced little fruit—so what! It doesn't mean that there isn't enough fruit in the world; it means that you *believe* there isn't enough fruit in the world. So perhaps it's time to work on your roots so you can believe there is plenty of fruit.

The belief in lack is predominant. You have learned to believe in lack, and you can learn to believe in abundance of every kind as well. Every time you see this belief made manifest in your life, you must continue to reprogram it and affirm the experience you want to have. *Let go of the belief in lack; it doesn't serve you or others. It limits your ability to give, which limits your ability to receive.*

As I looked at the receipt that popped out of the ATM, I couldn't believe what I was seeing: Unavailable funds. It showed a balance of negative $165.00! How could that be? (I soon discovered that a few weeks prior I had left my card in the machine, someone had used it to pull out $200, and I had promptly accumulated over $160 in bank charges for insufficient funds.)

I scrambled to find our other accounts to transfer money into the problem account and couldn't find the checkbooks or information. I went to another bank and found my ATM card didn't work. It was one thing after another this particular day, one money blunder after another, and the universe seemed to be mirroring back to me a definite belief in lack. I had not had this experience for many years and it brought back many earlier experiences of fear and lack.

I began to feel my fear and realize that this experience wasn't real, but it was bringing up in me the last remnants of a belief in lack so that I could let it go and reprogram a new belief, one of abundance and plenty.

I began to pray loudly as I drove from bank to bank to handle this business, in what I call my Scarlett O'Hara prayer, "With God as my witness, I will never be poor again!" I began to claim and declare that I was to be prosperous, and provided for, and that I would always have plenty of money to handle my needs!

I felt empowered as I moved through this experience, refusing to see the events I was experiencing as the truth of who I was. As I finally got the monies transferred and handled, I went to Pier One and ceremonially bought three lovely candles and a beautiful plate to set them on in my home. These candles would serve to remind me, every time I looked at them, that I lived in abundance and I was surrounded by beauty. I would never again believe in lack.

How to recognize when this unhealthy belief is triggered:

An event happens in your life that triggers feelings of fear, anxiety, terror, jealousy, or pain. You believe there is not enough of something that you need to feel secure. Your mind will work overtime to blame others or shame yourself. All of these tactics simply serve to avoid the real issue.

Remember, it is your belief in lack that is being triggered, and the only reason it is happening is so you can begin to reprogram your beliefs. Believing in lack doesn't serve you or the universe. **Hasn't a belief in lack caused you enough pain?** Remember, your perception of any experience is colored by your beliefs. Having a million dollars in the bank may seem like abundance to you, but Donald Trump would feel broke!

Reprogram your perception! You don't have to perceive experience from a viewpoint determined by a belief in lack. Everything that happens is just an experience. It is your belief that give it meaning. Remember:

> *Nothing has meaning except the meaning you give it.*

Take the pain of the moment and transmute that strong, powerful energy into creating a new belief system.

Affirm with energy:

> *I allow this experience to happen without believing in lack of any kind. I can observe this apparent condition without judgment. I watch this experience with detached observation knowing that I give it all the meaning it has. All the love, money, and health that I need is available to me so I know everything is working out for my highest good.*
>
> *I refuse to believe in lack of any kind! I refuse to accept this experience of lack as real or meaningful, except as an opportunity to reprogram my beliefs! I believe in abundance of every kind and absolutely refuse to believe that my good comes to me through any source other than the Universe.*
>
> *The universe provides many channels for my good, be it money, love, or success, and I trust the universe to create perfect circumstances in my life. I take responsibility for my beliefs and reprogram them now! I am worthy to receive, and I believe in a world of plenty. All that I need is always provided!*

3. Money is evil

There is a collective belief that money is evil or sinful. Ever heard, "It's easier for a camel to go through the eye of a needle than it is for a rich man to go to heaven"? How about, "Rich people are greedy"? Money is nothing but energy and will flow to you, through you, and back again according to your beliefs. The belief that money is bad is established by parental and early-life modeling. Take a look at the experiences you remember around money as a child. I invite you to journal the thoughts and beliefs you have held about money:

- *What did you hear your parents say about money?*
- *How did they handle money and what model did they set for you in their use of it?*
- *What did they believe about money?*
- *How are your beliefs like theirs—or completely opposite?*

These questions, if you take time to answer them, will reveal to you many of your beliefs around money. As you begin to identify what some of your beliefs are, you can begin to consciously reprogram them. You can choose to operate differently around money, and think differently about money.

> I was ready for a new car. Everywhere I looked I saw a Lexus. I had loved them for years and wanted one, and at this time in my life I was ready for one. I was happily married, had been building my church as a minister, and it was time to replace my old car. I decided to begin creating my Lexus in Mind first. I would park next to a Lexus whenever I could, I would notice them on the road, I would decide what color and exactly which amenities I wanted.
>
> The first thought I became aware of was, *Should a minister drive a Lexus?* I noticed I had a lot of beliefs about what a minister

should drive and about what people would think. I began to get in touch with beliefs about abundance not being very spiritual.

I realized this belief wasn't working for me, so I began to affirm that it was perfectly okay for me to have a beautiful Lexus and that I could be spiritual and drive a luxury car. After a few months of creating it in mind, I had an impulse to drive over to the Lexus dealership. There on the lot was the car I had been visualizing. Right color, right features, right price. The minute I saw it, I knew it was mine. It took a week for my husband to know it—but that Lexus was soon mine!

How to recognize when this unhealthy belief is triggered

One way to recognize when this belief in lack is triggered is to look at your emotional responses to an experience you may have around money. For example, if you have an opportunity to make more money, you may begin to feel some resistance. If you have a belief that having money is somehow *bad*, and you know you want to be a *good* person, you will find ways to sabotage your success. If you listen carefully to what messages you are telling yourself, you may hear thoughts like, *It's not spiritual to have money*, or *People with money are dishonest and corrupt*, or *What will people think of me? People will think I'm greedy*, and so forth. What are you telling yourself?

Your conflicting beliefs are sabotaging your harvest season. It's time to reprogram this false belief, one that has been handed down generation after generation, before you hand it down to your children!

Having more money only makes you more of what you already are. If you are a greedy person, with more money, you'll be more greedy. If you are a good, kind, and compassionate person, you'll be more so with a lot of money, and you'll have the means to do more good. If you relate to this belief that money is evil, just *get over it* and choose a new belief. After all, the world really needs a lot more kind, compassionate people with money! Why not be one of them?

> Nothing has meaning except the meaning you give it.

Affirm with energy:

I let go of all judgment around money. Money is simply money; it has only the meaning that I give it! I now give it a new meaning. It's good for me to have money; money is spiritual, and so am I. I let go of the belief that there is anything wrong with having money, and I allow money to flow freely in my life.

I do not worry about other's beliefs; I focus on choosing my new beliefs around money now! I am free to accept money and be paid well for my services. I let go of all beliefs that put a wedge between me and money, and I accept more of it into my life now. I am a money magnet. There is nothing wrong with me and money walking hand-in-hand, and I let go of all beliefs that would argue with this truth. The old beliefs no longer serve me, and I release them now! I love money and money loves me!

4. My good is dependent upon others

As children we were dependent upon the adults around us for everything. We grew and became more self-reliant, but now we can still unconsciously be setting ourselves up for disappointment and blame because we believe that our good is dependent upon someone external to us, rather than on our own supportive beliefs.

Your fruits are a result of your roots, and it makes sense that if you're not having the fruits you want in your life, you need to work on your roots, not on the people in your life! They are not your problem! **Others are not the source of your happiness.** Your job is not the source of your money; your mate is not the source of your self-esteem; your children are not the source of your love; **YOU ARE**. They are all channels of your good, but they are not the source. **Your connection to the highest truth you can contain is your source.** Work on the roots, for it is your roots that provide the fruits!

When my husband and I got married we decided to sell my house and move into his. It was our plan that eventually we would buy a new house together. Eventually, I felt the time had come! He did not. My soul craved a home of our own, that we had chosen together. He couldn't have cared less and resisted all action toward fulfilling my desire.

At one point I remember getting very angry and upset because of his unwillingness to even look at the possibilities. I felt utterly powerless, and a deep pain began to well up in me. This time, however, I was willing to accept this pain as an indicator of an unsupportive belief that was operating in me. I felt that realizing my dreams was up to him, and I needed him to provide my happiness. I finally was willing to look for the meaning underneath my pain.

I recognized a pattern in my life. I had looked to men as my source. I had lived powerlessly waiting for some man to save me and give me the fulfillment of the dreams in my heart. I remembered my father promising me wonderful things and then changing his mind, and the pain and disappointment that I felt. If Dad changed his mind—and he always did—I wouldn't get what I wanted. Everything depended upon him, his mood, and how many sales he made that week. I had continually played out this pattern: waiting, hoping, trying to please, anything—so that the man in my life would give me the fulfillment of my dreams.

I decided to reprogram this belief. I did not work on my husband. (Are you paying attention, ladies?) Instead, I worked on myself and my pattern of believing. I began to reprogram that belief by affirming that my source was not outside of myself, and claiming that this old belief no longer needed to operate in me. I began to affirm that my consciousness of good is my source, and all my deepest desires unfold through whatever channels the Universe chooses! I began to repetitively visualize the home of my dreams, the Mediterranean design, the palm trees out front, the pool, the tile roof, everything! I released the dream into the hands of the Universe to bring it about and I let my husband off the hook.

Guess what? Within a few months we had purchased the home of my dreams, just like the picture in my mind. I didn't have to manipulate my husband or fight and scream; it just worked out. It was important for me to follow my dreams. It was also important to recognize that my husband was not my source!

How to recognize when this unhealthy belief is triggered:

Believing that your good is dependent on others is triggered when you don't get some perceived good from somebody else and you are left feeling hurt, disappointed, or afraid. This belief, when triggered, can cause a great deal of fear and pain. **Remember, your perception of any experience is colored by your beliefs.** You don't have to believe that someone else is your source when some good is withheld. Everything that happens is just an experience. It is your beliefs that give it meaning.

> *Nothing has meaning except the meaning you give it.*

You reprogram your perception by knowing that your good is not dependent upon anyone else; it is between you and the Universe. **Work on your roots. The universe, through law, can give only according to your roots, or your beliefs.** The oak tree's roots continue to grow a strong oak tree. You may go over and pray that these oak roots grow an apple tree, but it's not going to happen. The Universe operates by the law of cause and effect, and for you to live optimally, you must operate in accordance with certain Universal Laws and Principles.

Affirm with energy:

> *I do not have to see this experience from a viewpoint determined by lack. Even if it appears that the good is taken from me, the experience has only the meaning I give it. My good can never be taken away from me. My good is not dependent upon any person, place, or thing. I am established in all that I need right now—if not from this channel, then from another!*
>
> *God is my source of everything, and no matter what is going on in my life right now, I depend upon my true source of support in all ways! These old beliefs have no place in me. I rely upon a higher authority for all of my good, and I am complete in myself!*

5. I have to be perfect

This one is really a belief in imperfection. You may believe in imperfection so much that you need perfection in you and others in order to feel okay. Perfection will never happen! The belief in needing to be perfect will cripple your ability to take any action in life and will create difficulties in your relationships. **Life is a process of correction and re-correction.** Even man's mission to the moon was off course 97% of the time. Like of all of life, it was a process of correction and re-correction.

How to recognize when this unhealthy belief is triggered:

When you make a mistake and you are crippled with grief, just know you have this belief that you have to be perfect operating in you. When others criticize you, and the criticism for you is very painful, know that you have this belief operating in you. When you stress out yourself and others to create situations that are impossible to maintain, know that this belief is operating in you. This belief is causing havoc in your life. Know that the pain it is causing far outweighs the effort it takes to reprogram it.

See the connection between the pain and this belief. Remember, you can still want what you want, and you can still excel in life; the problem comes with your out-of-control demands for perfection. Reprogram your perception, which is a demand for perfection! You don't have to perceive experience from a viewpoint determined by a need for perfection. Everything that happens is just an experience. It is your beliefs that give it meaning. When this belief that you have to be perfect is triggered, use the energy of the pain to reprogram the belief with intensity.

> *Nothing has meaning except the meaning you give it.*

Affirm with energy:

> *I can make mistakes and still be loved and acceptable. I can screw up and still be okay. Everything does not have to be perfect because I don't know what perfect looks like. Everything already is perfect just the way it is. I can accept what is for now. I let go of my need to be perfect, to look good, and to gain approval from others. I accept what is for now, and I relax and know that this is what my universe looks like today.*

6. I need others' approval

Needing others' approval is a program most people experience and operate on. As children we did lots of things to get approval from our parents. That behavior is natural. If we didn't get a sense that we were loved unconditionally, no matter what we did or didn't do, we became approval seekers. Why? Perhaps we have mistaken approval for love.

This endless seeking of approval from others can become a big problem. It causes us pain. It stops us from following our dreams. It interferes with our ability to lead effectively. It creates the experience of powerlessness. It totally screws up relationships. Seeking approval, we are dependent upon the whims of others, or what we imagine they would say or do.

Understand that what you really want is unconditional love, and you must give it to yourself first before anyone else will. You must reprogram your belief that approval is love. It isn't. It is only approval. Approval comes and goes; it doesn't mean anything except what we believe it means.

> I had been a minister for only a short time when I attended a wonderfully stimulating spiritual conference. I felt free of fear and excited about some new things to bring home to my spiritual

> community. One of the things I brought was some new music. I gathered a group of people together and taught them the new songs—heart-opening, uplifting songs—at least, I thought so. The day came that we would present these new songs at church. Many of us sang with joy, as we clapped and felt the spirit in this music. I found out later that many others did not like the new music one little bit. I had no idea that people could get so upset over a change of music. I was devastated and crushed. My belief that approval meant love was triggered and my perception created feelings of rejection, of not being loved and accepted. When I found out I didn't have the approval I thought I had, I was deflated

How to recognize when this unhealthy belief is triggered:

When you don't get the approval you crave from someone else, this belief that you need others' approval will be triggered. When you do something in order to seek approval (love) and you don't get it, this belief will be triggered and you will feel pain, shame, or stress. When you begin to step out in life and create positive change, this belief will be triggered.

You will experience a great deal of fear; after all, *you could lose the approval of others.* Such an experience of fear is mirroring your belief that you need to please others. Your fear, anger, and frustration will reveal to you where you have needed others' approval.

Reprogram your perception! You don't need to have another's approval to be loved. People can reject you and you don't need to have their approval. What others do is all about them and their beliefs! Why do you think it's all about you? What others think about you is none of your concern. Your only concern is your beliefs, and you must know that you are unconditionally lovable because you exist.

You don't have to perceive certain experiences from a viewpoint determined by needing approval. Everything that happens is just an experience. It is your beliefs that give it meaning. Begin to transmute that fear, anger, and frustration immediately!

> *Nothing has meaning except the meaning you give it.*

Affirm with energy:

> *I can experience so-called rejection without pain. I don't need to get others' approval in order to be loved. I am loved whether or not anyone approves of me. I don't need anyone else's approval to be loved and successful in life. I make clear and conscious decisions using the wisdom that is mine. I bless others and their opinions, and I stay focused in my life. I let go of my need for approval as it no longer serves me. I give myself the approval I desire. I am ready to live, love, and create magnificently; I allow others to have their own experience.*

7. I am separate from God/the Universe

This is the ultimate belief that creates all of our pain. It is the work of your soul to return to God, return to Love, return to Wholeness. The ego's work is to continue the belief in separateness, and the soul's journey is to return home. This belief in separateness is at the core of all the rest of the beliefs that cause you pain because it convinces you that you are separate from your Source, and separation is pain.

As you begin to reprogram the beliefs that have caused you pain, you will begin to reveal the truth of who you really are. If a person is steeped in self-degrading thoughts and beliefs, they are not going to be able to experience spiritual wholeness to the degree they could if they were mentally and emotionally healthy. A person is spiritual, mental, emotional, and physical: everything is connected. You are a whole being that cannot be separated. Your healthy beliefs affect everything. Your connection with God/Source/the Universe is directly related to your healthy or unhealthy belief systems. **Your roots produce your fruits.**

The most powerful practice that you can develop to further experience this oneness, unity, and wholeness is meditation. Through meditation you are able to align with this place of wholeness which automatically begins to reprogram your use of Mind, not through active affirmation, but by absolute alignment. There is more about meditation in Chapter Six.

It is your mind and its ridiculous regurgitation of dysfunctional thoughts that create so much havoc in your life; it makes sense that in quieting the mind through meditation, real and lasting change begins to take root in you.

Affirm in the silence of your soul, over and over again, until it begins to affirm to you ...

I am one ... I am one ... I am one ...

> *I am One with All That Is. I let go of all belief in separation and know that God, the Source of my love, my life, my light, my joy, my abundance, my everything, is right here where I am. I can never be separated from God. God is omnipresent and is right here where I am. This is the only truth—everything else I make up.*

Your perception of any experience is colored by your beliefs. You must reprogram your perception! You don't have to perceive experience from a viewpoint determined by beliefs that don't serve your highest joy, purpose, and abundance. Everything that happens is just an experience. It is your beliefs that give it meaning.

You can choose new beliefs. Use the power of repetition to daily stay conscious, and choose the beliefs that will create the life you want. In the next chapter you will discover the secrets to living in bliss more continuously and experiencing more life, abundance, and joy! Such a life is your inherent right!

CHAPTER FOUR

DISCOVER THE SECRETS TO LIVING IN BLISS

As you've heard by now, it is important to understand that your experiences and perceptions in life are a result of your internal programming and stored beliefs. Because of this internal programming, you experience life from different states of awareness, or consciousness. Your purpose is to evolve, to grow, and to live from higher states of consciousness more consistently. The lower states of consciousness were developed for survival in the jungle states of our evolution; in today's world, they only cause stress, pain, and suffering.

When you live from higher states of consciousness, you experience more joy, empowerment, love, and harmony. *You begin to flow with life rather than fight it.* It's like floating down the river rather than swimming upstream. You are full of energy, creativity, and life. Living this way is your Spirit's natural state.

Our whole purpose is to evolve to a state in which we are not constantly struggling, fighting, protecting, and surviving, but *thriving*. We are thriving when we are living in harmony with the energy of Divine Intelligence, the harmony that is happening in higher states of consciousness.

Stop surviving and start thriving

The following analogy is one of the most profound descriptions for self-understanding and self-awareness that I have ever experienced. For me and my students, it has become a tool to instantly understand where our awareness is and to be able to know when unsupportive beliefs are operating and what to do about them. It is a simple system. Your comprehension and practice of it can evolve your perceptions and experiences and assist you in living in greater joy, happiness, and success in your life. *I cannot overemphasize this!*

This system evolved personally for me from the genius writings of the late Ken Keyes and his best-selling book, *Handbook to Higher Consciousness*, which I recommend to all of my students. In that book, he discusses the levels of consciousness or awareness that we live in at any given time. I have taken that idea further and used the imagery of floors in a house to represent levels of consciousness.

- Imagine that your awareness is like a house, not just any house but a very large house.
- Imagine that you are seven stories high.
- Imagine that each floor gives you a different viewpoint when you look out.

Your viewpoint, or perception, is entirely different at each floor, and what makes it different is your own internal programming.

The bottom three floors represent states of consciousness that seek to guard and protect, sensually excite, and have power and control. These are the ego's main goals. These states have been humanity's main survival mechanisms since we first became conscious beings. While these states worked well when we were in the jungle just trying to survive, they don't work well as our awakening spiritual urges seek to express greater peace, joy, and true abundance.

Unfortunately, most people have so many inherited and conditioned patterns that hold them to the bottom floors that they feel helpless in climbing off the treadmill of pain, suffering, and lack. It doesn't need to be that way!

When people wake up to the HUGE AWARENESS that it is their own programming that is keeping them stuck and then begin to reprogram their beliefs, they begin to move upstairs to live a life of greater joy and happiness. The four higher floors represent a new consciousness, that of the *awakened soul*.

You live life from the higher floors when you begin to have more programming that is in alignment with unconditional love, abundance, and wholeness rather than the collective beliefs in separation, suffering, and lack.

Which would you rather have?

Read carefully, for the more you understand this idea, the more you can create loving, empowered belief systems that result in a life of peaceful, loving, and joyful perceptions.

It is also important to understand that there is nothing wrong with experiencing all of the levels of consciousness. *You will.* Because of your internal programming, you have been more magnetized to certain levels, and you will learn

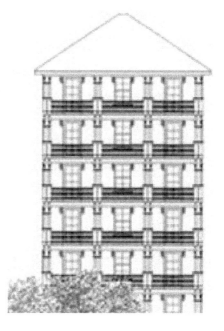

through repetition to live at a higher level, but understand that it is *all* a part of your life experience.

Understand your house of consciousness and bring freedom

Level One – The Security Center

Imagine the first floor of your house as the Security Center, also known as Level One. When you view life from the filters of Level One, you are preoccupied with money, food, shelter, others' approval, or whatever you equate with your personal security. This internal programming forces you to continuously battle to get enough from the world in order to feel secure. Some of the feelings associated with Level One are fear, anxiety, discomfort, grief, sadness, and even sheer terror.

Your internal programming may go something like this:

> *I feel secure when I have plenty of money or a good job; people must like me and must not criticize me, and I need their approval. I have a lot of rules about what I need in order to feel secure. When these rules are broken and life doesn't give me exactly what I need to feel secure, I experience suffering.*
>
> **What is it that makes you feel secure?**
> **What do you need to have happen in order to feel secure?**

These rules are all beliefs. You suffer when your self-imposed requirements are not met. When the outside world does not conform to your security programming (what you *must have* to feel secure), you will experience a trip to the first floor.

For example, if a person was criticized at work, and their internal programming suggests that criticism means a withdrawal of love or the possibility of the loss of job or financial security, then they will automatically go to Level One, or to the first floor. They will feel defensive and fearful and will overreact because of their internal programming, not because of the experience. *It is our internal programming that creates our reactions.*

Our internal programming can be changed, but not until we are ready and willing to accept that it needs to change, that it has caused enough suffering. Then we begin to do the repetitive practices that will change our program. In this example, if this person could begin to talk to themselves in a new way, they would begin changing their internal programming and, therefore, begin changing their experience.

Reprogramming suggestions:

> ***I don't have to experience fear when I get criticized. I can be criticized and still be loved and secure. I am secure in who I am, whether I am criticized or not. I can accept what is happening without feeling insecure. I am safe and secure. I am loved.***

KEY

Your state of consciousness is not determined by what is going on around you, but by what you are internally telling yourself about what is going on around you.

Level Two – The Sensations Center

The second floor of your house is the Floor of Sensations. When you view life from the filters of Level Two, you see life as happy and satisfying only when the physical senses are satisfied and stimulated.

You create circumstances and set up situations so that you can constantly be satisfied sensually. However, when things don't happen the way you want, you experience dissatisfaction, frustration, even anger and unhappiness. On this floor your stored belief systems tell you that to feel happy, you must have certain physical sensations. You will do everything you can to have pleasurable experiences such as good food, drink, sex, nice clothes, music, and things that please the five physical senses.

There's nothing wrong with experiencing pleasurable sensations; yet when our internal programming tells us that it is through physical sensation that we experience love, happiness, and success, we are left disappointed and empty. Some of the feelings associated with Level Two are disappointment, frustration, anxiety, jealousy, irritation, and boredom.

Your internal programming may go something like this:
I must have pleasurable sensations in order to be happy and satisfied. I will do anything I can to get them. If I don't get them, I don't feel loved. I need external circumstances to make me feel loved and approved. I need approval from others. I feel loved and comforted when I eat, drink, or have sex.

> It was Saturday afternoon, and Sally was planning on going out on a date with Jim that evening. Sally was excited and looked forward to being with Jim as he was someone she really cared about. They had been dating for over a month and things were progressing wonderfully in their new relationship.

> Unexpectedly, Jim called and was unable to keep their date that evening.
>
> When the date was cancelled, Sally's internal programming began to work overtime. Rather than simply hearing that Jim was unable to get together, her mind began to regurgitate all kinds of stories: *His excuse is pretty flimsy. How could he do that to me?* She began to feel unlovable, undesirable, rejected, and abandoned.
>
> None of these thoughts were factual; it was her internal programming that was causing her suffering. Instead of dealing with the real issue of her internal programming, Sally began to overeat, drink, and attempt to fill her emptiness with other sensually stimulating activities.

Reprogramming suggestions:

> *I do not have to feel rejected and unloved when plans change. I accept what is for now and know that I am lovable and complete. I don't look to others to fill my love supply, for I know that I am enough right now. I allow others the freedom to make their own choices, and I take responsibility for my own feelings. I am whole and complete right now.*

Level Three – The Power Center

The third floor of your house is the Power Center. It hosts all the belief systems that you store in order to feel powerful and influential and to have control in your life. You may store lots of ideas here about what you need to do in order to feel in control of life. You may force, push, and control others so that you are feeling comfortable and in control.

The more beliefs you store about how things have to go in life in order for you to feel powerful, the more you will have to go to the third floor to visit. When you have a lot of demands in life that everything go your way in order for you to feel powerful, in control, and on top of things, you will get to go here often. Sometimes it's easy to get stuck on the third floor because it can feel very empowering, and you can imagine you can literally force your way to the top. In the long run, this tactic will not work for you, as you can never power your way into the true happiness your soul seeks. Some of the feelings associated with Level Three are anger, annoyance, anxiousness, irritation, self-righteousness, and indignation.

Your internal programming may go something like this:

I must have power over others in order to feel successful. I have to be the smartest, and things have to go my way. I can't be wrong. I must look good, be smart, and know more than anyone else. My identity is determined by my influence and my power over others. I have a strong will; I choose what I want and I always get it. I will do whatever it takes to get what I want.

> The marketing team of a national organization is sitting around the conference table discussing ideas for a new product line. Barbara, the team leader, is bright, articulate, and accustomed to being right. She leads off with an idea she thinks is brilliant.
>
> Jeff, a new member of the team, cannot see the brilliance in her idea and begins to let her know in a tactful and professional way.
>
> Barbara flies off the handle, surprising Jeff, who hasn't yet learned not to disagree with her. Barbara takes disagreement as criticism and begins to power her way through the meeting, until all creativity is stifled and the meeting is over

Barbara has a lot of internal programming on the third floor that demands that she needs to be right and in control. If others disagree with her, it triggers her insecurities, and her perceptions are altered and her reactions overblown. She will do whatever she can to intimidate and control in order for those insecurities not to be triggered. The problem with this behavior is that it will not produce lasting success or friendships. In fact, it will kill relationships. Only when she begins to link her suffering with her addictive behavior and decides she has suffered enough will she begin to change.

Reprogramming suggestions:

> *I can experience disagreement or criticism without creating undue stress and strain. Others can agree with me or not and I can still remain at peace. I don't have to be right all the time; I can allow others the space to be heard as well. I let go of my need to look good under every circumstance, and I let go of my need to win at all costs. I am able to be successful and productive in a way that is helpful and beneficial to all. I am at peace in all circumstances.*

Each of these bottom three floors hosts belief systems that tell you that you need outer circumstances, people, and events to go a certain way in order for you to feel secure, happy, or empowered. *You will never experience true happiness while living only on the bottom three floors of your house, even though your ego will try to convince you otherwise.* As you look out of the windows of the bottom three floors, your perceptions of fulfillment will be met only if the circumstances you see match your internal programming.

How often do you think that is going to happen? Do you want your state of being to be determined by other people, circumstances, and situations? How empowered would that make you?

As you may have noticed, most of humanity lives on the lower floors of their houses, regularly experiencing pain and suffering when their expectations are not met.

Get upstairs!

In order to experience real happiness, joy, and abundance, you will have to move to the higher floors in your house. Let's take a look at those higher floors.

The higher floors of your house host belief systems that will create greater perceptions and experiences of peace, love, and true security in your life. On the upper floors of your house, you have clear access to Divine Intelligence, which dwells openly here. You hear guidance more freely and you are in tune with intuitive wisdom. Being on the higher floors of your house could be likened to a heaven-like state of consciousness. I like to think of living in higher states of consciousness as living in "heaven-on-earth."

Level Four – The Unconditional Love Center

The fourth floor of your house is the Love Floor. When you perceive life from Level Four, you experience unconditional acceptance, love, and feelings of joy. You experience this every time you choose to perceive life from the vantage point of unconditional loving acceptance.

It is very pleasurable on this floor, and you are able to interact with people with self-confidence while making few demands. You are not dependent upon others' actions, reactions, or approval on this floor. You are able to accept others as they are and accept yourself as you are, as well. You love yourself, you love others, and you experience significantly lower levels of stress.

When you look out the windows on the fourth floor, you perceive the experiences of life from the viewpoint of unconditional love, acceptance, compassion, and trust.

From the fourth level of awareness, your internal programming goes something like this: *I am lovable and acceptable just the way I am. I can love and accept others just the way they are. I do not need others to satisfy my inner demands but can accept what is. My happiness is not dependent upon outer situations and circumstances.*

Important Note: "Accepting what is" does not mean that you do not want changes in your life or that you live as a punching bag for anyone. When you let go of your unsupportive internal programming and repetitively replace it with supportive beliefs, you have more energy and creativity with which to demonstrate greater changes in your life.

Living in unconditional love means honoring yourself and making clear decisions in your life that honor everyone with whom you come into contact. It does not mean that you let others walk all over you or treat you badly. That would be called being a victim.

Level Five – The Penthouse

The fifth floor of your house is the Penthouse. When you perceive life from Level Five, you experience life as beautiful and abundant in every way, and everything works together in a synchronistic manner, unfolding whatever is needed easily and effortlessly.

Here, it is much like the fourth floor, but even better. As you symbolically look out the window of the fifth floor, or in other words, perceive life from Level-Five awareness, you see and experience the good unfolding. You live life with a sense of trust and wholeness, knowing that all is falling together for your highest good, no matter what is going on externally. You trust that even though things may go "bump in the night," all is unfolding for a greater good. You live in divine harmony; no matter what may be going on in the external world, the internal world is at peace and in harmony with a keen sense of abundance and beauty.

On this floor, life is experienced as a harmonious flow; there is a true sense of living in the present moment without needing to change anything or anyone. When experiencing life from the fifth floor, you trust what is and see the magnificence around you.

As on the fourth floor, you are connected to Divine Intelligence. You are aware that It is ever moving in and through you, guiding you to be at the perfect place at the perfect time. You are fully trusting that this Divine Intelligence is at work in others as well.

From the Fifth Level of awareness, your internal programming goes something like this: *Life is good. All things are unfolding for my highest good. I live in a world of abundance and beauty and I trust life. I go from good to greater good. God's life is my life now. I trust that I am a part of something whole, I am a part of the Divine Wisdom that is perfectly unfolding in all circumstances. I live actively, contributing to the greater good. I am a Creative Being and I am at all times conscious that I am creating from the highest place within me. No matter what appears around me, I rest assured that all is unfolding for the greater good of life.*

Level Six – The Divine Observatory

The sixth floor is known as the Divine Observatory. When you perceive life from Level Six, you experience life *as* the **Divine Observer**. You are able to watch yourself and others with a nonjudgmental attitude and with pure love. You are able to witness your visits to the lower floors of your house, and this witnessing will help prevent you from staying there long. The Divine Observatory is always open, always welcoming, and is always aware of its connection to the Divine Source.

When fully experiencing life from Level Six, you are experiencing life as one perfect event after another, without judgment or emotional reaction. You are not just connected to a Divine Intelligence, you begin to experience yourself *as **Divine Intelligence***, knowing and understanding that you are simply an instrument of this Intelligence. You truly understand that *nothing has meaning except the meaning you give it*. You let go of all judgment.

From the Level Six awareness, your internal programming goes something like this:

> ***There is One Life and that Life is God and I have my beingness in this life. I am not now, nor ever could I be, separated from this Life. Everyone is a part of God. I am not distracted by the dramas that I or others play out; I know that All is God.***

Level Seven – The Enlightenment Center

The seventh floor is the Floor of Enlightenment. When you perceive life from this center, you experience life as Infinite Intelligence does, seeing the unity and wholeness in all creation. **There is no separate identity. There is only the identity of the One—of Infinite Intelligence.**

Enlightened Masters such as Jesus, the Buddha, and many others have demonstrated this level of awareness for us beautifully. Today, in our modern world, thousands of people have had this enlightenment experience where they are opened at the seventh center and experience true reality. They may not stay there, but they have moments of insight after which they are never the same. I believe that it is humanity's great destiny to awaken to these higher centers and live this heaven-on-earth state of consciousness. That is the call to awakening.

As we strengthen our belief systems in oneness, life, love, peace, joy, abundance, and all of the qualities of God, the closer we get to the deeper reality of God: **God and I are one**. Through meditation and the repetitive practices of reconditioning the mind, we begin to align with the true part of ourselves and prepare ourselves energetically to meet our God.

The higher floors are where lasting peace, happiness, and abundance reside. We've heard, "Seek first the Kingdom of God and all else is added" and I say, "Seek first the higher floors and all else is attracted to us in divine harmony."

And so the big question is: *How does one live more from the higher floors than the lower floors?*

You must have more stored programming on the higher floors than on the lower floors. Wherever you have the most stored programming is where you will have to go. When your programming calls you to the first floor, it is calling you there to see what you have stored. You can either rant and rave, blame and victimize, or you can look at what's down there, choose to throw it out, and reprogram it. ***Through repetition you can choose the beliefs that are in harmony with the higher floors.***

Use these five powerful tools to raise consciousness

Use the following repetitive practices to build belief systems that will assist you in perceiving life as whole, perfect, and complete, aligning you with the higher levels of consciousness. Your deeply held beliefs attract like unto them.

1. Meditation

Practice disassociating from your busy mind and letting go of your judgment of everything. Practice the silent-mind techniques discussed in Chapter Six. Meditation automatically aligns you with the higher energies of the higher floors. *Meditation is the most important of all repetitive practices for storing programming in the higher centers.*

2. Repeat positive affirmations of the highest truth all the time

If you say over and over again, "I am abundant in every way," eventually you will start to believe it. If you say over and over again, "I am broke and I never have enough," you will believe that as well. More importantly, you will eventually manifest these chosen beliefs (and perhaps sooner than you expect). It's up to you. *What story will you tell yourself?*

3. Sleep-Repetition Learning

One reason I recommend sleep-repetition learning is because it *directly* influences the subconscious mind with a new belief. When the conscious mind is sleeping and *not arguing for limitation,* you go *directly* to the subconscious mind, reprogramming it with the ideas that you desire to reinforce, taking advantage of those unclaimed eight hours. It's easy to get in the necessary repetition, and it works.

4. Awareness and Understanding

Practicing awareness of any painful emotions can be a great tool for reprogramming the unsupportive belief systems that keep you stuck in lower states of consciousness. Awareness speeds up your own evolution and growth. There is more about this practice in Chapter Five.

5. Choose Your Environment

A wise sage once said, "Environment is stronger than will-power." Surrounding yourself with like-minded people and building a community around you that is in alignment with your highest dreams and goals makes a huge difference in your life. The community may be your immediate family, or you may need to create an extended family of friends that are uplifting, encouraging, enlightening, and supportive. The people you associate with have the most influence on you, like it or not. Don't blame them; start working on your own consciousness and beliefs. *Be open to attracting a new community of like-minded souls into your life.* Give yourself a strong support system!

Note: Many times in our intense spiritual work, we demonstrate struggle and pain as a way of clearing out what no longer works and revealing those places in us where unsupportive beliefs are operating. When you understand and can recognize this process for what it is, you can accept the feelings and move through them. In the next chapter, the information you will receive will shine the light on many of your deepest questions. Read it carefully, for it will give you the tools to recognize and reprogram your old beliefs as you learn how to turn your pain into your greatest gift.

CHAPTER FIVE

BREAK THE CYCLE

"*Life provides many opportunities,*" as Carl Jung once said, "to make the unconscious conscious," that is, to reveal to our conscious minds what we subconsciously believe. This is where real and lasting transformation happens—when the deeply held beliefs causing separation and fear are revealed, and we begin **consciously and *repetitively* to choose new beliefs**.

As we make this choice, we begin to break the cycle. Breaking the cycle of unconsciously chosen, unsupportive, and separating beliefs is mandatory if we are going to experience lasting transformation in any area of our life. Breaking the cycle means interrupting the automatic internal programming that simply reacts to life's experiences based upon the programming of the past. As we become aware of this natural process and how it works, we are able to break the cycle by choosing our thoughts, feelings, and perceptions.

Dr. Joseph Dispenza, a chiropractor and researcher of brain chemistry, talks about the relationship between our emotional patterns and the chemistry in the brain. In his work he explains that when we repeat an emotional pattern, our brains create webs of neurons and nerves, which are called neural nets. He writes:

Fortunately, it is possible to create new neural nets. It's all about making thoughtful, conscious choices instead of simply reacting through our old ones, usually made and embedded unconsciously. Make new choices often enough and strongly enough, and you'll override existing neural nets and create new ones. This is the reason why affirmations and visualizations can be so effective: by consciously creating new thoughts and imprinting them in our brain, we build new neural nets.

Let's imagine that your natural state is joy. Pretend that you live at Level Four or Five most of the time. Somewhere along the line in your day-to-day activities, something happens, and all of a sudden, you find yourself in fear, worry, and anxiety. You have triggered a trip to the first floor. You feel insecure, alone, and afraid. You don't feel God, faith, or any self-confidence.

You can just ignore your feelings and hope they will go away, or you can take the opportunity to heal and grow, and thus, move back up to Level Four and experience love and unity with Divine Intelligence. If you decide to heal and grow by practicing the methodology I am about to teach you, the next time something happens that triggers a trip to Level One, it won't trigger you as much—and one day it won't trigger you at all.

Welcome your pain and convert it to power

Understanding that painful emotional experiences are a sign of triggered belief systems that no longer serve you is a powerful step in beginning to recreate your life and experience lasting transformation. You can identify limiting beliefs and transform them into supportive ones by being willing to observe honestly what is happening within you. **We try so hard to justify, ignore, or deny our pain that we can miss the opportunity for healing—the very thing these unpleasant experiences are offering us.**

Your deeply held beliefs are revealed in many ways throughout your life. As was shown in the previous chapters, an event occurs and is perceived through the lens of your belief system; you automatically react in a painful way to this emotional experience. Now, you can choose to defend, justify, or blame. Or you can choose to get conscious by gaining the awareness and understanding of what your pain is revealing to you. After the awareness and understanding comes the conscious choice.

What follows is a powerful process for uncovering your belief systems and creating new ones. By paying attention to the painful emotional experiences we have, we can take the gift that they offer us. **That gift is powerful**. That gift reveals those areas in us that keep us separate, afraid, and lonely; and it enables us to choose to operate on the new internal programs of unity, love, and pure possibility. By being aware of our fearful and separating emotions, we can identify the beliefs that are causing the perception of separation, lack, and limitation.

For example, I used to be shy and extremely insecure. Whenever I found myself in new situations, I would begin to clam up, feel scared, and shut down to others. The more I began to be aware of this process, the more I recognized the subconscious thoughts that were operating within me. They created impossible standards for me to be happy and at ease, especially in new environments. I began to talk to myself in new ways and reprogram those old beliefs. I would tell myself: *I don't have to be scared in a new environment. I am safe and secure. I am good enough just the way I am. I don't have to look smart to others. I am good enough the way I am,* and so forth. By recognizing that our emotional reactions are simply signposts to our unconscious belief systems and to the filters through which we see life, we can use the principles of repetition to reprogram those old beliefs.

Christine was a forty-year-old divorced mother of two. She had been divorced for about two years when I worked with her. She was an attractive, warm, caring, creative woman, and a wonderful mother to her children. Although she enjoyed a supportive social life, she was not dating. She had a small business and she did well enough to support her children, buy a house, and live comfortably.

Then, Christine met John, whom she found captivating. When they first met, they had a great conversation. She didn't think anything of it and was actually surprised when he looked her up and called her. They emailed back and forth, had a few phone conversations, and planned to get together for a date. He was a very successful and intelligent businessman with a pleasant personality.

After their first couple of dates I got a call from Christine. Knowing she hadn't dated in some time, I was happy for her and anxious to hear how it was going with John. She told me that he was too old, she was no longer attracted to him, and he made her nervous. It sounded very different from a couple of days earlier, when she was telling me how interesting he was, and how she loved talking to him.

I knew there was more to this story. I could feel it in her voice. John had obviously triggered her fear, and she was putting up a wall around herself and making him appear to be the wrong man for her. This man represented many of the qualities Christine said she wanted in a relationship. Yet, when face-to-face with the possibility of having her desired relationship, she got scared; she was out of her comfort zone. I asked her a few more questions and it was obvious that she was in a great deal of pain over the situation. The next day she made an appointment to come and talk with me. She was wise enough to know that there was something in her that was calling out for healing.

Christine's ex-husband was very different from John. In fact, Paul was not successful; I would say that he spent most of his time making excuses for his lack of focus in life. He had no goals, and after several years of marriage, he and Christine were still renting an apartment with no hope of buying. He previously had held many low-paying jobs, seemed to attract one problem after another, and had basically chosen the role of victim in his life. He also had a problem with alcohol. Since becoming single, Christine had spent the last two years building her own business, raising her kids, and buying her first home. She was making a great deal of progress by herself.

Initially, Christine had a great time talking with John. As a business owner herself with goals and ambitions, she was stimulated by their conversation. She noticed, though, that the more she got to know John and the more she realized how smart and successful he was, the more she began to feel intimidated by him. She began to fear he would see through her, that he would see that she was not as together as she would have him believe. She even began to stumble over her words and feel insecure when they were together. She told herself that he was too old for her and she wasn't attracted to him. She did not want to see him again.

I explained to her that this wasn't about whether or not John was her type, her age requirement, or even whether or not she should go out with him again. His presence definitely triggered something in her. After all, she was the one in pain. If she ever wanted to be attracted to a successful and intelligent man, she needed to reprogram some old beliefs about who she was.

And so we began. I asked her to try to remember when she

first started getting triggered into fear. She described how they had been talking, and as she noticed how bright and articulate he was, instantly she began to feel insecure. The fear escalated as they spent more time together.

I asked her to go into that feeling and describe it, to be willing to feel it completely, to identify where it could be in her body. She held her hands under her heart, above her upper stomach.

At that point I asked her to recall a time in her past when she had had this feeling and to trust her own subconscious to reveal the appropriate experience which would eventually help her to heal. I asked her to simply answer yes, or no as I gently prodded her memory, "Was it before you were eighteen?"

She said, "Yes."

"Was it before you were twelve?"

"Yes."

"Was it before you were five?"

"No."

I then asked her to simply see if any memories came to mind of when she was between the ages of five and twelve that would help her heal today.

After a few moments she described her experience of starting school. She described herself as a shy little girl wearing a pretty dress, afraid to talk to others. She described an incident in which the teacher asked her a question that she could not answer and she was frightened.

All of the children laughed at her, and she felt stupid and afraid. She felt that because she didn't know the answer, nobody liked her. She decided then and there that she had to be smart or she was unlovable. She knew she was not smart enough. She wept as she felt the pain of this little girl again.

She had decided that people must never know she wasn't as smart as they were if she was to be accepted. I asked her to take this pain she felt in her chest and to allow it to gently flow to her hands, to hold it there, and describe it to me.

She described it as a big blob of gray matter.

I had her imagine that a large pink balloon began to encase it. That this pink balloon was filled with a purifying flame of cleansing energy and it was cleansing and healing this pain and the beliefs that created it.

She watched as the pink ballon purified and dissolved the gray matter until it became nothing and began to float up until it was out of sight. She began to breathe more deeply and feel lighter.

I then asked her to mentally float above the image of "little Christine," observe her, and give her permission to create a new story and a new belief system.

I spoke to little Christine; "You don't have to feel scared if you don't know the answer. It's okay. You don't have to know everything. It's okay for you not to know all the answers; you are still complete and happy and loved.

"Just because you don't know the answer doesn't mean there is something wrong with you. Even if others laugh at you, it doesn't mean that you are not loved and a wonderful person. You can be around intelligent people and feel secure; you are fine the way you are. You can be around successful people and feel secure.

"You are valuable just the way you are. Whether or not you make as much money as they do, you are as smart as they are. Your business is growing; you are fine the way you are. This belief you picked up long ago about not being smart enough and needing to know the answer no longer needs to govern your life, and you can release it. You are always good enough."

She began to feel the new belief, and then she began to claim it for herself.

> *"I am enough the way I am. I can feel secure around successful people. I can feel secure around successful men. I can be in a relationship with a successful, intelligent man, and I have a lot to offer someone that I choose. I let go of my fear and insecurities, and I let go of the need of being more intelligent. I am enough, just the way I am."*

After a period of time regularly working with this type of reprogramming, something powerful shifted. She told me that she began to feel the new inner reality, that she began to breathe deeply and feel very different. She felt at peace and could see herself conversing without trying to pretend she was ultra-intelligent and successful; she was much more relaxed and at ease with herself. Something had been healed.

What a gift Christine received because she was able to acknowledge her pain, gain awareness, and understand and reprogram her belief. Christine will need to be diligent in continuing the reprogramming and to consciously choose to look at her fears when they reveal themselves, before looking to blame others. In the past, she has been attracted to losers so that she could feel superior and her belief in her lack of intelligence wouldn't be triggered. Wouldn't it be better to do the work on reprogramming the old belief rather than spend years dating (or marrying!) losers? You'd think so, but most people don't do the work. A little personal responsibility now makes for a whole lot of happiness later.

Christine went on to go out with John a few more times

> without being triggered, but the relationship just didn't go any further. She got exactly the gift she needed from the friendship.

Embrace the transforming process

As you begin to work with the transforming process, you will notice huge changes in the way you perceive life, and then the circumstances you attract will be more supportive, life affirming, and will generate still greater success. You can utilize this process best at the point of the triggered emotional response. Use a journal to record your responses to triggered events.

1. Acknowledge your pain

Describe the situation that *first* triggered emotional pain (just the facts). Stay alert to when you first began to feel triggered. It may be subtle: for example, the feelings of uneasiness, insecurity, or boredom are a little harder to acknowledge than something obvious like anger, fear, or shame. The earlier we detect the trigger, the easier it is to identify what caused it.

2. Get awareness

Ask yourself, "What am I feeling?" (Denying and pushing away your feelings does not heal the unsupportive belief system.) You might feel *fearful, anxious, irritated, bored, lonely, sad, depressed, shameful, guilty, worried, angry, hurt, jealous, embarrassed, or disappointed.* Zero in on what you are feeling.

3. Get understanding

Ask yourself, "What level of consciousness am I in? To what floor have I gone?" This very act begins to clarify your experience. If you can see that you're feeling weak and afraid, you're probably visiting Level One.

Are you questioning your very security? Are you angry, upset, needing to be right, needing to have control, or needing to be perfect? You may be at Level Three, which is a good indicator of what beliefs may be operating. Becoming aware of the level begins to bring some clarity.

Continue to ask yourself questions in order to identify your beliefs. What meaning have you given your experiences that are causing you so much pain? Remember,

> *Nothing has meaning except the meaning you give it.*

Discover the belief system that is operating. In answering these questions, or more that come to you, you begin to discover a thought form, a belief, perhaps a repetitive experience from your past. If you keep asking, you will find. Your soul wants to heal and it responds to your questions.

4. Get busy reprogramming!

Reprogram the old belief by repetitively focusing and claiming a new supportive belief. Reprogramming is most effective when you have tapped into the deeper pain where you are experiencing the full effect of the unsupportive belief system. When you are able to take the energy of the pain and use it to forcefully *release* these old beliefs which no longer serve you, you can *claim* new ones! Now is the time to consciously reprogram those old beliefs. It's one thing to see your dysfunctions; it's another to consciously claim new programs in which to operate.

Taking responsibility for your emotions and getting the awareness and understanding, as well as doing the consistent work of reprogramming, makes a huge difference in your perceptions and experiences in life. It puts you back in the driver's seat, and gives you a powerful tool to reset your belief systems to support you in creating the life you want to live! It creates *lasting* transformation!

Reprogram your belief system

In my own life this process has assisted me in uncovering and reprogramming so many beliefs that were unconsciously running my life and affecting those around me. As parents, we pass on our beliefs to our children. We can do a great service to our children by reprogramming our beliefs, and sometimes it is just amazing to see how, as we heal our perceptions, our children automatically heal.

My oldest daughter Athena was to be married on a Sunday in May. On the evening before the wedding, Athena, my husband Mike, and Arielle, my twenty-three-year-old daughter, who lived out of town, were quietly discussing the next day. Suddenly, I realized I had forgotten to pick up Arielle's bridesmaid's dress. The bridal store was closed on Sunday, so there was no way to pick up the dress. My heart nearly stopped.

When I told Arielle, she began to cry, while looking at me with those sad eyes that seemed to say, *How could you forget me?*

I had been to that bridal store twice that week. Athena and all her other bridesmaids had just been there picking up their dresses; everyone had theirs, except Arielle.

Now, to say that I felt guilty, horrified, and upset was an understatement. To forget Arielle and to leave her out was exactly the opposite of what I had consciously been trying to do for her. Arielle had moved away from home at eighteen, and we had experienced four years of struggle in our relationship that was just coming to some renewal. So to forget her, leave her out, or have her stand out as "not-a-part-of" was unthinkable.

Later, I went to bed, but I could not sleep. I tossed and turned and kept thinking, What is the thought form around this experience? What is this pain I'm feeling? What am I telling myself that is creating this pain? What meaning am I giving this situation?

This time it was clear: it was a belief in separation, about not fitting in, about being different from the rest. It had showed up so many times in our relationship. In the middle of the night, I got up and went outside and sat under the bright and nearly full moon. I began to pray, then I began to cry, and I knew that there was a belief in me that I needed to heal. I knew this wasn't about the dress, but the situation offered the opportunity to heal something. I knew because of the intense pain I felt.

I gave up and surrendered all beliefs in me about separation, about not fitting in, about feeling disconnected from others. I began to claim and create a new belief system in me, in Arielle, or any other soul that wanted it! I prayed, affirmed, and reprogrammed the truth of oneness, fitting in, belonging, and being a part of the family. I had seen this old belief operating many times in Arielle and in myself, especially when I was younger, and I declared it healed now.

After a wild and howling night under the moon, I went back to bed and slept peacefully. Later the next morning, our work to find someone to open the store began. After four hours of searching, praying, knocking on doors, and trying all sorts of ideas, a coincidental meeting with split-second accuracy occurred, and the store was opened in order for us to get the dress. The wedding went beautifully, and Arielle experienced love and belonging, as we all did.

Our deeply held beliefs make themselves evident by various means. We transform these beliefs by taking advantage of the opportunity to release and reprogram new ones. When we experience painful times, and are willing to look at the beliefs that create the perception of separation or fear, we can begin to choose anew. This circumstance forced me to look at underlying beliefs and to do the inner work that was necessary to change those beliefs. Yes, we were able to experience the end result we had in mind, but even better than that, we were able to heal a belief that had created separation and distance between my daughter and me.

She had held a belief about being separate and different and not belonging to the family, which she had communicated to me many times, and she had created many opportunities to separate from her family, both physically and emotionally. I had to admit that I must have had something to do with her having that belief, and it was in me, too, so I promised myself that I would do my part to clear out the belief. That night, under the moon, I was able to experience a healing.

That's not the best part of the story. Two days after the wedding, she called to say that she had decided to move back home, find a new job and an apartment, and that she wanted to be closer to her family. Coincidence? I don't believe in coincidence; I believe in conscious cause. Choose a new cause, have a new effect. Radical, I know.

Choose to suffer or choose to be free

Only when we begin to realize that we have suffered enough will we begin to accept responsibility and do the transformational work of changing our belief systems. Only when we are ready to choose healing over suffering will we do the work. Ask yourself, next time you see a repeated pattern of suffering in your life, ***Do I want to suffer or do I want to be free?***

The following worksheet can be a tool for you to use when you are triggered. Use a journal to express your feelings, and allow your soul to guide you.

REPROGRAMMING WORKSHEET

1. Acknowledge the pain:
Describe the situation that *first* triggered emotional pain (just the facts).

_____
_____
_____

2. Get awareness:
Ask yourself, "What am I feeling?" You might feel *fearful, anxious, irritated, bored, lonely, sad, depressed, shameful, guilty, worried, angry, hurt, jealous, embarrassed, or disappointed.*

_____
_____
_____

3. Get Understanding:
Ask yourself, "What level of consciousness am I in?" What floor have I gone to?

Self Questioning:
    What am I telling myself that produces this emotion?
    What do I need to happen for me to feel okay?
    What meaning am I giving this situation?

What am I demanding in order to feel happy and enough? (a) Of myself? (b) Of others and the outside world?

Remember:

> Nothing has meaning except the meaning you give it.

Discover the false belief system that is causing your discomfort.

4. Get busy reprogramming!
Reprogram the old belief by repetitively focusing and claiming a new supportive belief.

I am whole and complete right now, in this and all circumstances. I do not have to perceive life this way; I choose a new belief.

Come up with your own new affirmations:

_____
_____
_____
_____
_____
_____
_____
_____
_____
_____

Accept responsibility for your emotions, transform your life

One of the most powerful and productive transformation practices is to accept total responsibility for your own emotions. Your emotions are the result of what you are thinking and perceiving both consciously and subconsciously when experiencing events in life. *As you honor these feelings and identify the thoughts behind them, you will see how your beliefs are creating your perceptions.* If you choose, you can then reprogram your subconscious mind, changing your perceptions, changing your reactions, and changing your experience. Radical!

Self-discovery is a powerful habitual practice that becomes a way of life. The greatest help you can give yourself is being willing to take responsibility for your feelings and perceptions, not as a tool to beat yourself up, but as a way of embarking upon a journey of revealing the highest and the best in you.

These tools can help you tremendously in dealing with the painful times as they arise and taking the gift from them. For serious pain and deep unresolved childhood issues, you may want to seek professional help to assist you in your growth and recovery. When you are consistently on the first floor it is difficult to move up alone. You need someone who can see clearly and help you navigate the dark stairwells. *Ask your soul to guide you to the perfect person.*

Note: Whatever you put your attention on will increase. The above processes are best used on an "as needed" basis. If you are constantly seeking to reveal old patterns and grow through your pain, you will constantly experience the pain of growth. *Seek to know joy. Seek to love life. Seek to create and multiply God's life in all that you do. Seek to see the abundance all around you and attract it to you.*

Let your dreams be unleashed; you now have the tools to bring them about. Take time daily for choosing your life, choosing your feelings, and choosing your beliefs. If you don't, who will? In the next chapter you will learn how to let go of attachment to your thoughts through simple practices of meditation. Nothing is more powerful and necessary than using your power of choice to shut down the chattering mind and find inner peace and solitude. You will strengthen your roots with new awareness and enjoy the fruits of higher consciousness!

CHAPTER SIX

SIMPLIFY YOUR MEDITATION PRACTICE FOR LASTING TRANSFORMATION

Meditate to bring freedom from past beliefs

As a repetitive practice, meditation is the most powerful transformational tool there is. It clears the mind, both consciously and subconsciously, of the limiting patterns of thought that do not serve you. Meditation is a practice of letting go of the importance of thought, and it assists you in tapping into Divine Intelligence. Meditation clears unhealthy beliefs.

With regular practice of meditation, you will become more conscious of your thoughts. In developing the practice of observing your thoughts, you are able to detach from the rambling and sometimes chaotic stories that your mind creates. You witness the stories rather than live them; they are just thoughts with no meaning other than the meaning you give to them.

Meditation also develops the mental discipline necessary to be a conscious chooser in life. Meditation trains you to hold a focus, and the ability to focus is imperative if you wish to choose new thoughts and beliefs. You use your mind; it no longer uses you.

Meditation is one of the most effective practices there is to assist you in living in higher states of consciousness. When you align with Higher Mind through meditation, you automatically withdraw from lower mind (old unsupportive conditioning.) The more programming you have on the higher floors, the more you live there. *Meditation creates programming on the higher floors.*

Every time you meditate, you are literally unraveling the belief systems that keep you trapped on the lower floors, and you are awakening to the higher energies of the upper floors where *joy, peace, and abundance* abide. The more you live in the higher centers, the easier it is to put your attention on a desire and have it manifest.

Why? Because you are not bogged down with false belief systems, and you are a clearer channel for Infinite Goodness in all of Its forms. *This idea is extremely important.* Higher consciousness creates like unto it. It is well worth attention to your meditation practice to enjoy living more frequently in higher consciousness.

There are many different forms of meditation in many spiritual traditions, but meditation truly goes beyond any religious doctrine. It is a simple practice that is personal for you. For the purposes of this book, I share with you my simple practice. **Meditation is the most important practice because it will help you to up-level your consciousness** (move to the higher floors) **and live in peace, no matter what may be going on around you.**

No problem is ever solved at the level of consciousness at which it was created. We must uplift our consciousness to the level of the solution. *At higher levels of consciousness, the creations from your lower states cannot be sustained.*

> **KEY** 🗝️
>
> *Meditation is the most important practice we can adopt to grow in spiritual consciousness and have the lasting transformation we desire.*

Nothing has made such a significant difference in my life as developing a meditation practice. I had messed around with meditation for many years, but it was only after sustaining a daily practice for several months that I began to see and experience life from a whole new viewpoint. I began to comprehend things that I hadn't before understood. I began to see life more clearly. I began to have access to more creativity and inspiration, and little by little, the old programming began to lose its hold on me.

The important thing about meditation is that it needs to be a habit, *a practice which is done repetitively*. It is an investment that dishes up great dividends in peace, awareness, and a more joyful life. Here are just a few of the benefits that you will experience as you develop your meditation practice.

Ten measurable benefits of meditation

1. **It assists you in living in higher consciousness.** If you are not sure why that is a good thing, I suggest you read Chapter Four again, and ask yourself, "Where do I want to spend most of my time?"

2. **All knowledge, wisdom, and power is internally available.** When you begin to withdraw your constant attention from the relative, material-sense world through meditation, you begin to

open up to a whole new reality. In order to be able to comprehend many spiritual truths, your mind must be open and receptive to inner knowing. That doesn't come from anything external to you; it comes from your own knower within. If you're externally focused, you will miss out on much inner wisdom.

3. **You tap into a power for good.** Through meditation practices, you energize and build belief systems that are anchored in the higher spiritual centers, attracting greater good into your life.

4. **Creative Intelligence is available to you.** Through meditation you tap into the field of unlimited possibility, unity, wholeness, and peace. Creativity flourishes.

5. **Meditation assists you in living in greater peace and serenity.** Meditation allows your mind to rest, and hooks you into your innate peaceful presence. The peaceful perceptions continue beyond the twenty minutes or so you spend meditating, and this benefit is cumulative as you meditate regularly.

6. **You enjoy improved powers of concentration and intellectual development.** You develop a more-disciplined mind, imperative for living from choice.

7. **Meditation improves health and bodily functions.** There is a great deal of evidence that suggests that the body, mind, and emotions are all connected. Meditation helps release healing properties in the body for improved health.

8. **Meditation develops intuition and personal contact to your higher wisdom.** Intuition is available to everyone. It is a conscious contact with the knower within. A relaxed mind is more receptive to the impulses of intuition and sensitive to its urgings and guidance.

9. **Meditation clears the unhealthy beliefs and limiting patterns of thought that do not serve you.** Meditation shines the light within, and the darkness disappears.

10. **Your life gets better; it just does.** The more you are attuned to Universal Intelligence, the more you live in attunement with the higher energies of life. These frequencies simply create out of what they are: life, love, and abundance.

Note: Below are instructions for teaching yourself to meditate. You will derive much benefit from this "focus meditation." However, it would be to your advantage to learn meditation from a trained instructor, and I highly recommend doing so. There are centers in most large cities where you can learn Transcendental Meditation, Kriya Yoga, Zen, and any number of different types of meditation. It's good to have a personal instructor, who can also verify that you are meditating correctly and provide the encouragement and inspiration to keep up the practice. These meditation centers are also an excellent place to find a strong support system or circle of friends.

Easy meditation practices anyone can do

Focus Meditation. Find a comfortable chair where you can put your feet on the floor, sit with your back straight, and breathe comfortably.

You should be comfortable enough that you can withdraw your attention from your body. Take everything off your lap and rest your hands comfortably. Many people use different poses and positions, which are all good. Find something that works for you. The important thing is to meditate regularly, preferably at the same time each day.

First begin to notice your breath; watch it go in and out. As you do, you will begin to relax and center. After a few moments put your attention on the area around the middle of your forehead, between your eyebrows. This is where the seat of the sixth center of consciousness is. Simply concentrate on this area by holding your focus here. When your mind starts to wander, gently and easily bring it back to this point. Remember, where your attention goes, your energy flows. By continually focusing your attention in this sixth center, you are energizing and magnetizing it. Each time your mind wanders, and it will, bring your focus gently back to this point.

It also helps if you have a word or phrase that you can repeat silently over and over. This is called a *mantra*. This mantra gives the mind something to do. The mind likes to talk, so give it a word to repeat silently, and then when it starts to wander, simply bring the attention back to your word and focus on your forehead. I use words like "I Am," "Ah," or "Om." Find a word or phrase that works for you. It doesn't matter what the mantra is; you are only using it to hang your mind on for a while. Don't judge your wandering mind; observe it. You are detaching from the mind and experiencing that you are the witness, the knower.

All your meditation practice is perfect. There is no bad practice. All is effective. Some sessions feel better than others. Let go of all judgment around your meditation and it will help you let go of the judgments you make about yourself in other areas of your life!

Tips for successful meditation

Meditate in the same place everyday. You are practicing the principle of repetition and that practice alone will help your experience. You will build an energy that supports your practice.

Try to meditate at the same time every day. Look at your schedule and see where you can fit meditation into your life. I find that the first thing in the morning is best for me, before the affairs of the day start filling my mind and time. Some people enjoy the evening as well. Meditating morning *and* evening is even better.

Meditate with an empty stomach. You will find it more comfortable to meditate either *before* or a couple of hours *after* meals so that your body isn't busy digesting food.

Turn the phone off and close the door! Let members in your household know what you're doing and that you're not to be disturbed. It is essential that you not be interrupted. Know that you deserve this time to yourself.

Start with twenty minutes a day. It takes at least that much time to start to enjoy and settle into it, especially in the beginning. Trust me when I say it will be the most effective time of your day. Your mind will lie to you and tell you that you've got other things to do. Your mind will find reasons why you can't meditate; it will waste no time in telling you. Just thank it for sharing. It is not you. It is only a tool you use. Just laugh at it and remember how funny it is; silly mind!

> *I will lift up mine eyes unto the hills, from whence cometh my help.*
>
> —***Psalm 121:1***

In the next chapter you will learn some highly effective and easy-to-implement transformational practices that you can apply in your life starting today.

CHAPTER SEVEN

MAKE IT EASY BY MAKING IT A HABIT

Use repetition to be happy and free

What we do over and over again has the greatest impact on us. Therefore, we must listen, talk, and think about positive truths. There is a great and timeless truth given to us in that mystical, magical story, *Alice in Wonderland*: "Unless we change our direction we will wind up where we are headed."

The mind has an interesting quality; it acquires habits through the repetition of thoughts. We all have habits: successful people have developed successful habits, while positive people have developed positive habits. Habits can be acquired, changed, or dropped. Introduce a new thought over and over again; that thought then becomes an action; that action eventually becomes a habit.

Brushing your teeth had to become a habit—notice how it feels awkward to *not* brush your teeth? Clasp your hands together; see which thumb is up. Notice how familiar it is. Now shift all of your fingers up so that the other thumb now rests on top. Notice how that feels. It feels awkward to invite a habit to change, so you must use your will power continually in order to replace the old habit with a new one.

Likewise, a new thought must be introduced and reintroduced until that thought becomes an action. Whatever is worth being, doing, or having is worth these concerted efforts. Sadly, most people will simply tolerate lack, limitation, distress, and struggle rather than invest the needed energy and will power to realize positive change. Everything has a price, especially in the spiritual life, and it is our responsibility to elevate ourselves to an ever higher level of existence.

Being creatures of habit, we must consciously change our habits and make positive spiritual living a habit in order to deal most effectively with our problems and live as we truly desire. This change requires knowledge and action. The more we are exposed to spiritual knowledge and inspiration, the more this influx acts like clear water, cleansing our minds and flooding our consciousness with divine experience. Study and contemplate things of the spirit, and then act! The more we do, the more the old will fall away, and the new will take root. What we do over and over has the greatest impact.

In order to live in greater joy, happiness, and success, you must have more stored programming on the higher floors (higher centers of consciousness) than on the lower floors (lower centers of consciousness). Through positive habits of repetition, we can choose to align with the beliefs that are in harmony with the higher floors. The following three practices, when repetitively chosen, begin to reinforce the beliefs that resonate with higher states of consciousness.

Three easy practices that work every time

1. Choose Gratitude

The most powerful practice we can use to transform our consciousness is the practice of gratitude. The practice of gratitude is not just about saying "thank you," but is about aligning with the power of Divine Intelligence.

By choosing the energy of gratitude, we automatically begin to lift our awareness. Our choice to experience the feelings of gratitude—no matter what is going on in our lives—begins to align our thoughts with a Higher Power. Gratitude is an experience that is chosen. It is a choice to live and move and have our being in the experience of *all is well*.

When we are truly experiencing gratitude, we automatically move upstairs! The term *upstairs*, as you may remember, is used to illustrate a state of higher consciousness. "Upstairs" is a state where you are more in tune with the higher energies of Universal Love. It is an experience of acceptance, where fear is not the guiding emotion, and a sense of trust pervades. There is the sense that *all is well*. There is the experience of unconditional love. There is the experience of everything unfolding exactly as it should. There is the experience of synchronicity and abundance.

Choosing gratitude is a powerful practice in uplifting consciousness. In the New Testament, Paul said, "Be ye grateful in all things." That's in *all* things. In the midst of whatever is going on, we can make the choice for gratitude. Remember, a state of gratitude is not dependent upon everything going as we think it should. A state of gratitude is a choice we make, moment by moment.

2. Choose Joy

The practice of choosing joy is a lot like gratitude; it is a conscious choice. It is a choice that doesn't rely upon external circumstances. I do a practice in my classes where I ask my students to pair up and share with their partner a remembered experience when they were feeling joy. As they are sharing, they get excited, happy, joyful—they begin to feel great.

Nothing has changed in the room or in their lives, except that they made a conscious decision to feel, share, and experience joy. The energy in the room has shifted. Everyone feels uplifted. They move up to higher levels of consciousness. They didn't all of a sudden inherit money; their lives didn't change externally. Their attention is the only thing that has shifted.

At anytime, we can begin to choose joy. Right now, think of a time when you were in complete joy. Allow yourself to ponder it. Allow your body to breathe it and to feel overcome by it. Notice, how do you feel? If you were able to do it, you automatically began to move up in consciousness to the higher floors. You now feel more loving, more connected, and more in tune with Infinite Wholeness.

If not, try it again! Choosing joy is a choice to move upstairs to higher consciousness. We demonstrate greater life, abundance, joy, and love from the higher floors. When our goal in life is to live on the higher floors, we will do so. We will begin to free ourselves from the grip that our lower-level addictive belief systems have on us, and we will more and more often consciously choose the *all is well* mind-set.

3. Choose Beauty

Choosing to see beauty is another practice that automatically lifts awareness. God is beauty. Every time we look for beauty and see it, we move up in consciousness.

Take a walk and allow yourself to quietly ponder the simple beauty you see all around you. Notice the color and depth of nature; the forms, structures, and designs; the personalities, their variety and expressions. See the beauty all around you, and you begin to see God all around you.

When you begin to see God all around you, you begin to experience God in and through you. As you do this, you cannot stay stuck in the basement. Seeing beauty lifts consciousness, lifts awareness, and entitles us to experience the bliss of the Divine. Seeing beauty is a practice that can be made into a habit.

What will *you* see? Our habits of choice will determine the life we see and the life we experience. Even in the middle of life's challenges and struggles, we can begin to use these practices to experience gratitude, joy, and beauty. We are learning to create life from the inside out and to use practices that will become habits which will create a life we love living.

What we say to ourselves can set us free or hold us in bondage

We become what we say to ourselves all day long. Have you ever really listened to yourself? Would we talk to others the way we talk to ourselves? As we become aware of the critical voice inside our heads, we can say, "Stop!" Then we choose again. Consciously choosing gratitude, joy, and beauty will lift our awareness to the higher side of life. That choice to lift our awareness to the higher side of life will automatically cause us to begin to create from the higher side of life.

> **KEY**
>
> *The Psalmist said, "Set a watch, O Lord, before my mouth; keep the door of my lips."*
>
> **Never say a thing about yourself that you do not want to see realized in your life.**

Suppose that a recorder were strapped on your shoulders the first thing tomorrow morning and you carried it with you all day until the last thing tomorrow night. Suppose that it recorded every word you said, and then those words were repeated to you. You might be a little embarrassed; but more importantly, would those be the words that you want creating your life? Never forget that the circumstances of your life tomorrow are molded by your mental conduct today.

> *So shall my word be that goeth forth out of my mouth; it shall not return unto me void.* —Isaiah

Is this what we want to claim for ourselves? As we listen to what we are saying to ourselves and others, we can also ask, "Is this what I want to create?" We can then begin to think, speak, and discuss what we want to create, not what we don't want to create. We have a fun little habit in our family. When someone starts complaining, one of us will say, "Is that what you want to create?" It stops us in our tracks, or at least makes us aware of what we're doing. Do you talk more about what you want to create, or more about the problems you see?

Praise and honor yourself

What we tell ourselves builds beliefs. We can develop habits of praising ourselves, just as we may have developed habits of criticizing ourselves. It is a matter of choice. When we've done something that we wish we hadn't done, we have two choices: we can belittle ourselves by going over and over the situation in our minds, or we can say something like, "I'll do it better next time. I'm learning to make new choices and the past is over. Wow, I'm really growing."

The first choice drains our energy, ruins our day, and actually attracts the opportunity to screw up again—because we're focusing on it. Or, we can forgive ourselves and get on with life.

By choosing the latter, we move up in consciousness to a higher floor where, in the future, we'll be able to see more clearly and choose a better choice of action. Praise and honor yourself in all situations. If you get a little voice in your head that says, *I shouldn't praise myself, that's egotistical*, get over it! If we don't start praising and honoring ourselves, we're going to get stuck on the lower levels (lower consciousness), and it's just one big drag there.

What are our words empowering? They are empowering whatever we are talking about. If we want to empower life, love, and happiness, we had better start talking about them, and find some other people to listen. If we want to empower ourselves to live life from a place of greater success, joy, and beauty, we need to start thinking, reading, and listening to ideas about them as much as possible all day long. I know that the world does not support this kind of thinking. I know people who say snidely, "Oh isn't that sweet, let's be positive." But in reality very few people have the discipline to look beyond the external events and take responsibility for their own perceptions and choices.

The news corporations make a ton of money by broadcasting the most horrific events they can find. Pain sells better than happiness. We are being bombarded by the worst of the worst on every channel and throughout every medium. It is not easy to stay above it when we are engulfed in it. Such a constant barrage of negativity will drain our energy, and it will cost us our dreams.

We must train our minds to see beauty, joy, and abundance in life if we are going to experience them. The world needs people to choose more joy, beauty, and abundance. We don't serve the world by buying into its unhappiness, lack, and distress. We serve the world by being willing to go above the negative; for only by going above it can we lift up others.

Make your choices for positive repetition a lifestyle practice that will lift your awareness and keep you centered. We need *you* to play along. But you need to know that there may be people who will not support you in this lofty goal. That's okay, do it anyway. When your life gets better, they may just ask for your help—or not.

Twenty surefire and easy ways to transform your life

Hooking up positive repetitive practices with already established practices makes it easy to build new supportive habits. Start listening to positive, uplifting, and inspiring audio programs and music that support your dreams and goals. Read inspiring biographies, or watch them on TV. Keep the rest of your television diet positive and uplifting. The internet is a great new source of inspirational material. You can log onto my website at **www.janettemariefreeman.com** for many positive resources. Books and audio products are available at your local library as well.

Add the following practices into your regular daily schedule for remarkable results!

1. **While sleeping:** Get eight hours of positive programming easily by listening to sleep-repetition CDs.

2. **While exercising:** Listen to positive material or uplifting music. If exercising outside, look for the beauty everywhere you go. Get in a rhythm with affirmations, i.e., "I am strong, I am fit, I am strong, I am fit …"

3. **While getting ready for work:** Have something positive playing in the background. Pump yourself up by talking to yourself in ways that elevate your consciousness and set the tone for the day. "Today I will have a great day. I am intelligent and wise in all that I do. I attract great opportunities for success and I am a blessing to others."

4. **Before you walk out the door, get in the habit of affirming:** "Everywhere I go today I am surrounded by light, protected, and

blessed. I attract great opportunities for success." Yes, go right ahead and say it out loud.

5. **Driving the kids to school:** Take time to talk to them in positive ways, affirming the good for the day. Encourage them to choose to see the best. Look for beauty along the way. With small children in the car, play games looking for all the beautiful things they can see. It elevates everyone's consciousness!

6. **Driving or riding the train or bus to or from work:** Listen to positive, inspirational material, read books, etc. Affirm, "I ride with safety, and this train is taking me to even greater success. Everywhere I go something great is happening. Wherever I am, God is, and all is well."

7. **Stopping at stop signs or lights:** Say to yourself, "I stop doing what no longer serves me." With green lights say, "I move forward in life with success and joy."

8. **Phone rings:** "Life calling with more great news."

9. **Picking up the mail:** "More money and opportunities keep coming to me."

10. **Picking up the newspaper:** "More good news. Every time I turn around I hear good news."

11. **Paying your bills:** "I am so grateful to have money to pay these bills. Every time I pay out, more money comes back to me. I am rich. Thank you, God!"

12. **With every donation, gift, or tip given:** "Everything I give comes back to me multiplied 100 times!"

13. **Every time you find a penny, nickel, dime, or money of any kind:** "Thank you. My good just keeps coming in! I am a money magnet."

14. **With every bit of money or good that comes in your life, no matter how big or little:** "I am a magnet for all kinds of good. It keeps finding me!"

15. **Every time you see something you would like to have or see someone experiencing some good in their life:** Praise it and bless it. "That's for me, too!" Whatever you praise and bless is attracted to you!

16. **When something good happens to you:** Be *overly* grateful, praise it, and affirm that this is what you expect. "I expect the good to come to me! That's for me!"

17. **In the midst of a challenge or struggle:** "This too will pass. I know that all the solutions I need are already at work."

18. **When you pay too much for something or lose something, rather than bemoaning it, say:** "Thank God I'm rich!"

19. **When something unexpected changes in a seemingly difficult way:** "With every closed door, another one opens."

20. **If you start to catch a cold:** "I'm catching a healing. I release that which no longer serves me."

These are a few ideas and you can add to this list. There are plenty of opportunities in your life—start looking for and claiming the good you want to experience. Make it a lifetime practice.

> **KEY**
> *If your friends aren't making fun of you for being so positive, you're not being positive enough!*

In the next chapter you will learn how to unlock your greater possibilities and allow your dreams to come true!

CHAPTER EIGHT

UNLOCK GREATER POSSIBILITIES

Explore and discover your innate genius

Before any lasting transformation takes place in a person's life, there must be a desire for that change and a dedicated decision to accept it. Whether we seek success, happiness, or greater peace, we must have a strong and powerful desire for it. We must have a big enough reason in order to be willing to *go the distance.*

We are all called to explore and discover our innate genius. I believe that you, too, have that inner urge for more: to be more, to experience more, and to express more. It's part of the creative urge inherent in all of us. The Divine Creative Nature only knows creation. It must multiply itself.

The more we know ourselves as a part of this Nature, the more this creative urge calls us. In fact, It calls us at the depth of our being. Will we deny it out of fear, or will we give it the nourishment it needs to burst into form? Only through enough repetitive attention will this voice have a chance to be heard, take root, and begin to grow the fruits of our souls' desires.

Have you ever asked yourself, *What would I do if I won the lottery?* Of course you have. If you allowed yourself to think about what it would be like to give money away, buy what you wanted, do work you wanted, give back to the community, or whatever it was for you, there is a definite sense of excitement. It's not about the lottery because the lottery is not the only way it can come to you; *it is about allowing yourself to dream.*

Unfortunately, most people don't allow themselves to dream very big. They don't even allow themselves to ponder questions like the lottery question for long because it's not likely to happen. You've got to have a dream in order to have a dream come true, but too many times we get too bogged down to even allow ourselves to ponder, *What would I really like to experience in my life? What would I like my life to be like? What would I really like to be, to do, to have? How do I want to be remembered?* If we don't ponder these questions and have a dream and a vision, then we miss out on living a dream-filled, powerfully purposeful life.

> *You are, that you might have joy, and have it more abundantly. – Jesus*

Dare to dream in order to have a dream come true

Many people don't allow themselves to dream because they think they have to know how to *make the dream come true*. We don't do it, we attract it. The dream pulls us toward it when we can consistently and repetitively hold it in mind. The clearer the vision, the more energy there is for manifestation. We need a dream that excites us, one that will propel us through the fear that comes with it.

> As a young, struggling single mother in dead-end jobs, I had a vision. That vision was written down endless times in endless ways, and I have the journals to prove it. It was visualized, hoped for, prayed for, and yes, even begged for. It made my heart sing and excited me to think about it. I loved hearing motivational speakers tell me that my dreams could come true. I sought them out; I wanted to be inspired and I wanted to remember that it was possible. Because when I looked around at my life, I could only wonder how I dared to have such a dream—after all, it was the furthest thing from my reality. I dreamed that I would marry a wonderful man, that our family would be close, and life would be fun. I dreamed that I could travel the world. I dreamed that one day I could be a minister, an author, a teacher. I dreamed that I would have abundance in every way and live a life of peace and spiritual harmony.

I repeat: My life was far from this reality. I wasn't even close to having a wonderful husband—no, not even close! I was in classes for many years learning about principles that would qualify me for the ministry, but I was not a likely candidate. I wanted to travel the world, but my trips mostly consisted of the four-hour drive from LA to Fresno on about fifty dollars for the weekend, including gas.

My point is this: I had a big vision before I had the means to see how it could happen. The other point is that my vision excited me. It was what I wanted, and nothing would satisfy me but the vision. It pulled me. There was no other choice for me; it was my destiny, and I could feel it. I wanted this dream so much that I wouldn't give up because there was just no other choice. That's the kind of desire that makes big dreams become reality.

The desire must be strong enough to carry us beyond our fears and discomfort. When the desire is strong, it will carry us through our fears, our setbacks, and our problems along the way. The desire must be strong enough for us to hold on to when all else looks like it's falling apart.

There are a lot of wants along the road in life—yes, I want this and that, so do you—*but I'm talking about something deeper: a deep desire, a deep urging for greater expression.* Desire is the first step in creation. The universe continues to say "yes" to our *deeply held beliefs* about our desires, and when we hold onto the desires, even though it seems like forever, everything unfolds in perfectly right timing.

When was the last time you allowed yourself to dream big and choose what you wanted to create in your life? What does your soul call you to?

I believe that as we evolve spiritually, the Infinite Nature of the Universe within us urges us to expand, express, and create.

What calls you to greater love? What makes your heart sing? What fills you with delight? Why not choose to experience it? What would you need to believe about yourself, your life, or your opportunities in order to manifest this dream? *That's the key. What would you need to believe?*

As a young mother with a big dream, I knew that I needed to keep believing in myself and keep growing the beliefs and support within myself in order to find myself worthy of my dreams. My work was on myself, not on the world around me. Oh yes, I tried to find a husband, don't get me wrong. But over and over again, I learned that *I manifested not what I wanted, but what I subconsciously believed.*

For example, even when I said I wanted to find a great guy and get married, I kept attracting unavailable men. I wrote that I wanted commitment. I said that it was what I wanted; I could convince anyone of that. But guess what? The fact was, the men I was most interested in all turned out to be unavailable, either emotionally or physically, or not able to commit for a number of reasons.

I had to get real. I manifested not what I wanted, but what I believed. I must have not been willing to commit myself. How could I blame men, or complain, "There are no good men anywhere"?

When you start to take responsibility for your life, it can be very bothersome; it's just so much easier to blame others. However, if you want changes in your life and lasting transformation, you eventually have to take responsibility for your beliefs and do the work required to change them. And guess what? I had to do it more than once. I had to start saying "no" to what I didn't want and saying "yes" to what I did want. It didn't feel natural either, by the way—change usually doesn't.

When you have a vision to pull you, you will keep on track. When you don't have a vision to pull you, you just go around in circles. That gets old fast; the scenery doesn't change much.

This mating-game part of my vision didn't materialize quickly for me. I had a lot of work to do within me before I could accept a new marriage. In fact, I was single for exactly twelve years.

After about eight years, I found a wonderful man with whom I fell in love. There was only one problem: he lived four hours away from me, and we had no long-term future together. We had different visions for our future. I justified the obvious differences for two years, making excuses and looking at the short-term pleasures rather than the long-term vision. I hoped that it would be different, but all along I knew that we would never have a future together.

It's painful when you try to put a square peg in a round hole. It's painful when you try to make something work that never will. It doesn't mean that there's anything wrong with either of you; you just don't share the same vision!

I had to get clear on what I wanted to have in my life. I had to be willing to say "no" to what I didn't want in order to make room for what I did want. I had to make a stand in my own being, to say what my vision was and that I would make the decisions that supported it. I wanted marriage, family, and a beautiful home, and that was not going to happen in this present situation. I prayed, I cried, and I surrendered: *God, I don't know how to do this, help me do it differently.*

By the way, I prayed this more than once. I continued to hold in mind my dream and my desire, and I surrendered the way, the means, and the method to Divine right action. I continued to affirm: *I deserve and accept a committed relationship.* Two weeks after breaking up with my long-distance love, I met the man that would be my husband. Did I recognize him as that? Oh, my, no! As you know, I still had some more work to do on me.

> *What do you want?*
> *What does your soul ache for?*
> *Allow yourself to dream.*
> *Don't forget to write it down—more than once.*

Unleash the fourteen-hour commitment in your life and win

Lasting transformation calls for a deep commitment and requires a radical shift. Before any lasting change takes place in a person's life, there must be a desire for that change, and a dedicated decision to accept it. Whether one seeks success, love, happiness, or greater peace, there must be a commitment.

The fourteen-hour commitment is an incredibly effective, easily implemented practice of exposing yourself to massive amounts of positive material to create a change in your thinking and belief systems. Making a commitment to massive positive repetition practices can begin to transform your life immediately.

Fourteen hours a day equals over fifty percent of your daily twenty-four hours. When those hours are spent exposing yourself to positive input that supports your vision, awakening, and new expression, it is only a matter of time before you see powerful results.

In the first chapter, I introduced the idea of sleep-learning, which I will discuss further in our next chapter. *One third of our lives is spent sleeping. We can reclaim that lost time.* Through sleep-learning, we can go directly to our subconscious mind, bypassing the noisy conscious mind, and input positive instructions. While our conscious mind is asleep, the subconscious mind is not; it never sleeps. It simply receives the information you give it, without argument.

Remember the analogy I used earlier comparing the subconscious mind to the filing/storage room? It simply receives the information given it, stores it, and begins to create from that which is stored. We need to store new information more than once.

When we expose ourselves to positive material at night, our conscious mind doesn't interfere with or counteract the positive messages we are being given. In fact, right before we go to sleep and immediately upon awakening, as we hear the positive suggestions, we can instruct our subconscious mind to receive them and to begin immediately to act upon the given information! Remember: You are the driver! Sleep-learning is an easy way to reprogram the subconscious mind. It is easy to get in the habit of just listening while we sleep—all we have to do is turn on the machine.

Can you imagine taking the next year of your life just to incorporate this one thing into your daily routine? You would listen eight hours a night for 365 nights—2,920 hours of positive affirmations going directly to your subconscious mind and reprogramming you to accept greater good. Don't you think that might make an impact on you? You bet it would!

What if you did it for five years? That's 14,600 hours of transformational, powerful programming going directly into your subconscious mind. You're going to be sleeping anyway—why not take advantage of your down time and create some new beliefs that can transform your life for greater good? You can't lose. Just for fun, what if for the next ten years you incorporated this one practice into your life? That is 29,200 hours, or three and one third years of nothing but positive input.

What if small babies started their lives listening to such positive input and the early files of their storage rooms were full of positive, loving ideas and beliefs? They would unconsciously seek out matching experiences that mirror those early beliefs. Do you know any small children or babies that might benefit from sleep-learning?

So that takes care of eight hours in a twenty-four hour period. Easy enough, but what about the other six hours that make up fourteen hours in a day? You can spend six more hours in your day being exposed to positive, supportive information through listening to inspirational, motivational programs or uplifting, inspirational music; or reading inspirational, supportive material. That's six more hours spent exposing yourself to massive amounts of positive input that supports you, your vision, and your divine identity.

This doesn't mean that you have to stop everything; you can include these practices with what you are already doing. Listen to audio programs when you're getting ready for work, in the car, or around the house. Read positive supportive books rather than watching the tube. In Chapter Seven I gave you twenty ways to incorporate positive practices into your life. You can go to my website and hear uplifting messages on my e-radio, and also check out the sleep-learning CDs that are available. The massive amounts of repetition will create a change in you and will reprogram your subconscious mind.

I especially recommend massive repetition in those periods of your life when you are consciously choosing a new reality and needing to create the momentum to move out of your comfort zone. In those periods of your life, fear of the unknown will often stop you from moving through the change, and you will need extra help to get over the hump. The fourteen-hour commitment can provide that help. Simply make the commitment to sleep-repetition learning every night for eight hours and then spend an additional six hours a day exposing yourself to positive information.

It's like going on a physical training program: you get a trainer, go to the gym, eat very strictly, and monitor the results. It's not the same as a maintenance routine. When you're activating the Creative Principle and consciously choosing to create changes in yourself and your life, you need to focus intently on your goal. Massive repetition practices incorporating sleep-learning and day-time input will make an impact on you—they cannot help but do so!

Live your dreams! Choose what you want from your life! Choose to be all that you were created to be! Let the practices of positive repetition support you and your fullest expression. You were created to live, to love, and to be happy. Resolve today to let go of every single belief that argues with that most innate truth.

> **KEY**
> *Today, I dare to dream and open myself up to God's vision for my life. I am God's expression and was created to live life in joy and abundance. I accept and live this truth now. Every day I spend my time being reminded of this truth.*

Try the fourteen-hour commitment for twenty-one days. I promise you, you'll feel different. If you have a strong enough desire, you'll keep the commitment until you're living your dream. Of course, then you'll get another dream and do it again, and again. And you'll be happier, healthier, and wealthier.

In the next chapter, we will talk more about sleep-repetition learning.

CHAPTER NINE

REVOLUTIONARY RESULTS WITH SLEEP-REPETITION—THE EASY WAY

It's fast, easy, and effective

While sleep-repetition learning has been used effectively for years in improving school performance, learning languages, and training athletes, its regular use for personal growth has never been fully exploited for the tremendous value it can provide. Taking into account the nature of the subconscious mind and its ability to receive and store information, as well as its ability to cause people to attract circumstances into their lives, it's easy to see why sleep-repetition is so powerful.

Professor Leonid A. Bliznitchenko, Director of the Department of Experimental Phonetics at the Potebni Institute of Linguistics, wrote the following:

"Sleep-learning is a process that takes place during natural sleep. It consists of introducing into the human mind information which is processed and memorized while the student is asleep. The sleep-learning lesson begins while the student is in deep relaxation and continues after the onset of sleep."

Virtually every authority in the personal growth movement and educators of all kinds agree that repetition is necessary for learning. We learn through impact and repetition. You cannot control the impactful situations in your life, but you do have something to say about the repetition incorporated into your life.

The reason most people's efforts fail is that they lack the necessary repetition in their lives.

Why, if people know that repetition is necessary, do they fail to continue it? The answer is obvious: It gets boring. No one can affirm a thousand times a day, "I am prosperous in every way." We try it for a while, and then we give up.

We simply don't get the amount of positive repetition in our lives needed to create positive change. We are bombarded by negative media and fear-based thinking and attitudes, and the stressful realities of our lives are too consuming. We are, by default, exposed to substantial amounts of negative repetitive programming, and unless we do something to radically reverse that pattern, we are simply going to be living the results of this exposure.

We have to wake up! Most of the automatic thought patterns are a result of the stored belief systems and thought patterns in our subconscious minds. A few sporadic positive suggestions are not going to make an impact. If we want to snap out of the negative treadmill of automatic thinking and behavior, *we have to get the high level of positive repetition necessary to reprogram the subconscious mind.*

Our old patterns are grooves so deep that our daily conscious efforts are simply not enough to keep our motivation and interest sustained; we will give up when we don't see the results we need. It takes a committed decision to reprogram old patterns, and sleep-repetition learning is an easy commitment we can introduce into our lives as a pattern of practice, like brushing our teeth.

Sleep-learning is easy. One of the reasons I am so convinced of the effectiveness of sleep-learning is that it is easy enough to continue long-term and make into a habit. It doesn't get boring because it is a passive activity that does not require any discipline on our part besides turning on the CD player, and without effort we get eight hours of exposure and direct programming of the subconscious mind. Let's take a look at how it works.

I described earlier the very simplistic analogy of the subconscious mind as a storage system and creative center:

- It simply receives whatever information it is given and acts upon it.
- It does not judge and decide which information it will receive but receives everything.

Negative habits of thought will continue to program us for failure, illness, and lack. Have you ever observed what you think, or what you say? It is so common to say things like, "I can't, I'm not good enough, there's not enough for me," and so forth. Even when we are exposed to positive information, our conscious mind continues to argue if the positive information does not fit into our already-accepted beliefs.

However, while sleeping, the conscious mind is inactive, and it cannot argue with our positive input. So, as the files in the storage system that are holding positive, loving, supportive belief systems continue to get bigger, the files that hold the old negative, fear-based ideas continue to shrink for lack of input. *We must get conscious* about what we are inputting into that bio-computer called our mind. If we do not, we cannot blame another. The choice is up to us.

Sleep-learning is effective. The earliest modern reports on sleep-learning that I've found are rooted in the work of Vetterstrand in Germany in 1893, N.V. Viazemskii in Russia in 1903, and Frances Burdon in 1904. All used some form of suggestion during sleep on their patients. Later, people such as Hugo Gernsbach (June 1911 edition of "Modern Electronics"), and Aldous Huxley, *Brave New World*, speculated about what the future uses of sleep-learning might be. Twenty-six years later Huxley devoted an entire chapter to sleep-learning in his book, *Brave New World Revisited*, 1958.

Dr. Laverne C. Johnson of the United States Navy Medical Neuropsychiatric Research Unit summarized a review of the subject:

> *"Information processing during sleep is summarized, and published reports lead to the conclusion that the sleeping brain does receive, process, and even store information presented during sleep."*

There is ample research available for those who need more information to be convinced, but I'll bet, if you're anything like me, something in you knows that sleep-learning is worth a try—something in you knows that it makes sense. I encourage you to listen to your heart and realize that there is more to you than your accepted belief systems and that you need help to activate change. Modern technology makes it easier than ever to practice sleep-learning.

Starting the practice of sleep-learning

Sleep-learning basically consists of playing some kind of audio device all night while you sleep. You can choose from a number of sleep-learning audio programs or create one that affirms the ideas or beliefs that you want to program into your subconscious mind. The easiest way to do this is to have a CD or tape player in your bedroom that you use to play a CD or tape all night while you sleep.

Simply set the system to *Repeat All*. That's it. The volume that you select is up to you. I have found in the beginning, if you are not used to having noise in the background, you may need to have the volume quite low. That's all right; your subconscious mind hears at subliminal levels.

I prefer to hear what is being played at night: it is an excellent way to go to sleep—simply repeating the suggestions that you are hearing with your conscious mind, while affirming your *intention* to be reprogrammed and to accept the suggestions into your subconscious mind.

As you awaken in the morning, the suggestions are the first thing you become conscious of, allowing you to consciously affirm these new ideas and enabling your conscious mind to work in harmony with your subconscious mind.

At any rate, you may need to get used to the process. If it is new for you to have some noise going on in the room, the CD may awaken you in the beginning. Most people find that if they awaken in the night, they simply use that time to affirm the positive suggestions they are hearing, falling back to sleep soon afterwards. Feel free to turn the volume down as you are getting used to it.

What if your mate doesn't want to listen? Many people have this dilemma: one person wants to listen and one doesn't. Simply turning the volume lower may solve the problem while allowing your partner to benefit from the sleep-learning. Perhaps if they understood the benefits, they would be more willing to try the process. Other people have found that listening through headphones is a workable solution.

I had this problem in the beginning with my husband. He didn't want to have any noise in the background, saying that it woke him up in the middle of the night. Since it was my voice on the CD, he would wake up thinking I was speaking to him! As I helped him understand the benefits of sleep-learning in a way that interested him (*He* would be more successful in *his* work), he adjusted to it and doesn't complain. I've noticed he sleeps just as hard as he ever did and snores just as loud!

Proven secrets can do wonders for children

Many busy, caring parents feel guilty for not spending enough quality time with their children. Now, parents can simply play a CD and know their children are getting eight hours of continuous, positive input for building supportive, loving belief systems.

One of the challenges that faces most parents is not having as much time as they would like for giving their children positive reinforcement. It is not that they don't want to; it's that they are usually stressed out from their own jobs, work, or the cares of the day.

> I remember when my children were little, as a single mother of three, I would come home tired and ragged by the end of the long day. Too many times the first words out of my mouth were something about the kitchen being a mess or the chores not being done. Even in my more conscious times, it seemed as though there was little time for the high level of positive reinforcement my children needed as they were formulating their early beliefs about themselves. For my children, there was just too much time in front of the TV. I know the frustrations that we, as parents, feel and our guilt for doing less than we know we should.
>
> My motivation in making these positive tapes for my own children when they were small was, quite frankly, to offset my guilt. I felt good about playing positive, loving affirmations for them while they slept. I knew they would get eight hours of positive input, which felt very good to me as I tucked them in, with hugs and prayers, and turned on the tape machine. (My nineteen-year-old son and twenty-three year-old daughter still listen to my sleep-learning CDs; it's a habit!)

Now, I don't believe that sleep-learning will raise a child. Nor do I believe that parents can treat their child with disrespect or offer constant devaluing messages of unworthiness and expect these recorded positive messages to have a great influence on the child. One's daily example has the greatest impact on one's children. However, there are other factors that can make a difference, and sleep-learning can assist parents in offsetting the negative influences around their children and help them cope with the everyday stresses of parenting.

Most children today face massive amounts of exposure to the negative influx and pressures of today's world. As much as parents try to protect their children, television, movies, music, outdoor advertising, and peer pressures are too much for them to combat. Combine that with the fact that most parents are experiencing a great deal of stress in their own lives, stress that cannot help but be passed on to their children.

When we understand that the early belief systems accepted by a child begin to attract the experiences in life that mirror his or her beliefs, we begin to see how important it is to help establish positive and empowering belief systems at an early age. Those early beliefs attract like unto them.

One analogy that has always helped me to understand this is to imagine that every time a thought is experienced, it makes a small groove in the brain. When new information is experienced that matches that thought, it is attracted to that groove, making it a bit deeper. As that groove becomes more etched into our brains, it affects the very way we see and experience life, attracting to us the very experiences that help reinforce these grooves. Our entire perception of life is perceived according to which grooves are deepest.

When we were young, did we believe that we were loved, supported, and supplied for and that life was safe? If those were the deepest grooves, we began to attract experiences in life that mirrored those perceptions. If we were somehow taught that we were not supported or supplied for and that life was unsafe, we began to experience life from those eyes and continued to attract experiences that mirrored those early beliefs. The early-accepted beliefs attract like unto them, getting more and more established and, ultimately, becoming the law of life for us, as well as becoming our reality.

> When I was a little girl, I experienced regularly the wrath of an older brother. His taunts and verbal and physical abuse were extremely detrimental to this little one's perception of self. I remember beginning kindergarten as a shy little girl, convinced that I was fat and ugly and that no one would like me. (Of course, I was not fat and ugly!) With every encounter, I knew I would not be liked, and I was even convinced that the teacher didn't like me.
>
> This kind of thinking continued to haunt me for years, causing me to put on weight and hide away within myself. Now, would my experience have been different if I had been told repeatedly that I was beautiful, loved, and perfect just as I was? Of course! We know that the beliefs a child establishes early in life form the foundation from which they grow. This is not rocket science. It is much easier to reinforce positive programming early in life rather than try to change it twenty, thirty, or forty years later.

Sleep-learning is incredibly effective for babies and children of all ages, the younger the better. They are not so much reprogramming old beliefs as establishing early operating programs for life. Additionally, if they develop the habit of listening to positive programming while they sleep, they will not want to go to sleep without it. In my experience, along with that of other mothers, the habit of sleep-learning acts as a sleep trigger. It's like Pavlov's dogs. After the parent establishes the pattern of turning the CD on, tucking the children in bed, and allowing them to fall asleep hearing the soft, soothing messages, the children formulate a pattern for going to sleep. Soon, this repetitive pattern for going to bed is established, and they will fall asleep quickly. Every parent that I've spoken to about this reports that their children, who once had so many excuses for not going to bed, can't wait to tuck themselves in and turn on their CD. They go to sleep faster and sleep more soundly. During the day they are repeating the positive affirmations they are hearing at night and are showing signs of being more at peace with themselves.

> My own son is a perfect example of this. When he was born nineteen years ago, I played tapes on the millionaire mindset for him. I played the tapes on auto reverse, and they played all night, every night, for at least a year. As he grew up he was one of those kids that always had money; he attracted money like a magnet.
>
> Even as a very young boy of five or six, he showed this ability. When we would go to the grocery store, he would guess what the total amount would be and was always within a couple of dollars. He knew how much everything cost and would analyze everything in terms of financial value. As a nineteen-year-old he is well on his way to becoming a multi-millionaire. His maturity around money is phenomenal and he understands true prosperity principles, demonstrated by the fact that he always tithes 10% to his church and manages and invests his money wisely.

Use sleep-repetition to make you happy, healthy, and wealthy

Sleep-repetition is a learning tool that you can use to help reprogram your subconscious mind. You can purchase ready-made CDs specifically designed for sleep-learning, or you can make your own—just find ones you will listen to repetitively as a pattern. Especially effective are affirmative suggestions that are spoken in the first person.

For example, "As I sleep I hear these suggestions, and I am open and receptive to them. I am wealthy in every way."

Many people enjoy playing motivational material; yet I have found it can disturb my sleep. I prefer soothing, no-beat music with softly spoken affirmative suggestions. The music helps the body relax and magnifies the message of the spoken word. Music has been shown to assist learning in many ways. At the end of this book I have included templates for making your own sleep-learning CDs at home using your own recording devices (See page ??). Of course, you don't need a template; simply record the affirmations and suggestions you want to adopt.

These repetitive practices are most effective when the person doing them has an intention to shift, grow, or change. It is your *intention* that will make the biggest difference. Your intention to reprogram your beliefs will begin to shift and reinforce what you are hearing at night; your intention will help reinforce the new beliefs during the day; your intention will assist you in maintaining the practice as a consistent and repetitive habit. It will be the easiest habit you ever acquire. Just do it. Again and again.

As you turn the page you will realize that your destiny is truly in your hands. Moment by moment you can choose a new reality. The past is behind you. This is a new day.

> **KEY**
>
> *To know that you are the chooser is to be master of your fate.*

CHAPTER TEN

LASTING TRANSFORMATION IS YOURS

Be the master of your fate

By radically participating in life, taking responsibility for your feelings, and looking at your experiences as effects instead of causes, you begin to create the life you want. Is it easy all the time? Of course not. It requires your willingness to face your deepest fears and not run away. To be a master of your fate, you choose again and again, day after day; you continually choose what it is you believe.

Maxwell Maltz, the author of the classic book *Psychocybernetics* wrote,

> *One of the reasons it has seemed so difficult for a person to change his habits, his personality, or his way of life, has been that heretofore nearly all efforts at change have been directed to the circumference of the self, so to speak, rather than to the center.*

So many times when we try to improve our lives, we try to fix something externally: get a new job, a new mate, a new house, etc. The efforts at change are directed to the circumference of ourselves rather than the center. It's human nature to try just rearranging our effects. However, we have learned that any lasting transformation has to have its point of origin at the center (or hub) of our being, rather than at the circumference (or rim) of our lives.

In other words, a new cause has to be established—a new belief system must be known and reprogrammed in order to reinforce a new effect that is sustainable. It took many years to build our current set of beliefs, so changing and raising them to higher levels will take repeated reinforcement of the new ideas.

Lasting transformation doesn't occur just because we want it to. It requires putting forth the sustained intention to know something new. A fad diet of a few affirmations will not create lasting changes, but a lifestyle of positive, repetitive habits will.

I have had many experiences of working on the inside to create the changes on the outside. I know that only inner transformation can create the lasting changes we desire. When I finally decided to develop my abilities to write and to take on the identity of an author, I needed to do a lot of work *on me* before I was able to accept this role, this choice. It did not come easily. There were more times than I care to count that I wanted to give up and tell myself that I could not do it.

What I know is that all that we need is within us, and we can begin to tap into that genius when we repetitively build the belief systems that allow it to come forth. This change comes through a conscious reprogramming of the self-condemnation and criticism habits. Choose over and over again to affirm and know that *all that you need to know is revealed to you now*. Empower your genius through affirmation and repetition. I don't think I could have continued this process had it not been for the conscious practices in my daily living as well as the multiplied effects of sleep-learning. Sleep-learning is the second most powerful tool I have discovered for self-transformation, and to think how easy it is just makes me laugh.

I love the writings of Walter Russell. In his classic book *The Man Who Tapped the Secrets of the Universe,* Glenn Clark writes about this remarkable man. Russell was a musician, composer, illustrator, painter, architect, sculptor, scientist, sports champion, figure skater, horseman, philosopher, and lecturer. He had no formal education after the age of ten, yet he accomplished more than most people ever dream of. When asked the secret of his success in life, he replied:

> *I believe sincerely that every person has consummate genius within him. Some appear to have it more than others only because they are aware of it more than others are, and the awareness or unawareness of it is what makes each one of them into masters or holds them down to mediocrity. I believe that mediocrity is self-inflicted and that genius is self-bestowed. Every successful person I ever have known, and I have known many, carries with him the key which unlocks that awareness and lets in the universal power that has made him into a master.*

He was asked, "And what is that key?"

> *That key is desire and trust. It is the search for greatness, for tapping into that genius and the trust to release it into the great eternal Energy of the Universe. Geniuses have learned how to gather thought energy together to use for transforming*

> *their conceptions into material forms. The thinking of creative and successful men and women is never exerted in any direction other than that intended.*

Our ability to think is what differentiates us from the other species who share our planet. It is our ability to think that allows us the power of choice, to choose who we are, what we will believe, and what we will become. Our ability to think does not guarantee that we will use it wisely, but we have been given the gift, and it is up to us to use it as we choose. Our basic and core beliefs are a result of what we think about most, and who and what we are exposed to regularly. *Who are you? Are you a limited human being or a Divine offspring with genius capacity?*

Know who are you and with whom you identify

> This is a fable about a large mountainside where an eagle's nest rested. The eagle's nest had four large eggs in it. One day an earthquake rocked the mountain, causing one of the eggs to roll down to a chicken farm in the valley below. Chickens, who are known to mother anything in the coop, sat on the egg until it hatched, and then raised the baby eagle with their chicks.
>
> The eagle pecked around like the chickens, played with the chickens, and believed she was a chicken. The eagle loved her home and family, but something in her spirit cried out for more. While playing on the farm, the eagle looked up to the skies above and noticed a group of mighty eagles soaring in the skies. "Oh," the eagled cried, "I wish that I could soar like those birds."
>
> The chickens laughed and pecked at her and said, "You cannot soar with those birds. You are a chicken and chickens do not soar. You will never be able to do that."

Something in that eagle wanted to fly so badly. She secretly dreamed she could fly, but when she mentioned it again, the chickens just scoffed at her.

One day as the eagle was pecking around in the barnyard, an eagle flew close by, staring at her. The eagle continued to come by, curious as to why an eagle was pecking around in the barnyard. Finally he stopped to talk to her. She was afraid, but her admiration for him won out, so she stayed and listened. The flying eagle asked her, "Why are you pecking around in this barnyard? Don't you know you are an eagle and eagles fly high in the sky?"

"Oh, no," she said, "I am a chicken, I cannot fly. I've always wanted to fly but I cannot fly." The eagle tried to convince her that she could, but finally gave up and flew away.

Later that night as the eagle rested in the chicken coop after all the chickens had gone to sleep, she began to think, *What if I could fly? What if that eagle was right? I don't look like a chicken ... maybe I could ... Oh, no, I could never do that.*

Well, this continued for some time, and every day the barnyard eagle would look up at the other eagles flying, and then look at the chickens pecking, and dream that one day she, too, would fly. When she went to bed she would fly in her dreams. This went on for months until one day, the soaring eagle returned.

Again he told her that she was more than just a chicken, and this time she was ready to believe. She had dreamed that she could fly, and now she knew she could not live her life without trying.

The eagle coaxed her to walk high up the mountain to the ledge, and from there she looked out at the valley below. Even though she was filled with fear and anticipation, she leaped off the side of the mountain, and as graceful as nature itself, she stretched out her wings and began to fly. Up and down she flew

> as she felt the wind rustling through her mighty feathers. The exhilaration was like nothing she had ever known before, yet as natural as life itself. She soared high above the barnyard below, crying out for her friends to notice her. But they couldn't see her; they were busy pecking at the ground.

Like the barnyard eagle, we are divine, unlimited beings, meant to soar. We can follow our dreams, the voice of inspiration that is calling us, and stretch our wings and take that leap of faith to a higher level of existence. *The choice is ours.*

A quick warning is necessary here. This story could have ended very differently, as it does for so many people. Knowing that we have divine potential and never utilizing it is a painful place to be. Had the eagle only wished for more and never taken any steps to manifest the dream—never taken the action necessary—she would have died in quiet desperation. She had to walk out of the barnyard! She had to jump off the ledge and into the unknown! She had to follow her mentor and trust.

If we have a dream for a greater life, we must be willing to commit to the repetitive practices that will change the belief systems we have accepted, and begin to create from the inside out the belief systems that will support us and our desired reality. We must think of ourselves as divine and whole, not as poor and limited. We must reprogram those old beliefs that keep us in limitation and misery. We must commit to repeatedly knowing the truth, not as a sporadic diet, but as a lasting practice of radical self-discovery.

We will be liberated from our fears only when we choose to focus on our brilliance. Our fears are like dragons, sneaking up and destroying our brightest dreams. Our fears are only thoughts, though, and they can be replaced by stronger, more powerful thoughts, repetitively chosen.

All the dreams in the world can bring us only discontent if we allow our fears to swallow them. The choice is ours.

Take responsibility, muster courage, and create joy

To those who can take responsibility for their feelings and experiences and muster the courage to try again come the greater spoils of joy, success, and happiness. The choice to continue to know a deeper truth, to move beyond our past perceptions, and to live anew will bring great rewards. The repetitive practices talked about in this book are powerful tools in creating lasting transformation. It is not just a diet of affirmations that will create the change, but a lifestyle of positive habits. As we monitor our thoughts and beliefs and choose to create new ones, we will be empowered and fulfilled. The person with strong, empowered belief systems will attract life's greatest opportunities and blessings. *Repetitive practices are the practices of empowered people.*

You must choose daily to expose yourself to the ideas, thoughts, and people that support your new version of yourself. We all need a community of like-minded people to play with, so that we may grow and stretch and feel supported in the process. These new friends, our co-creators, are out there if we look for them. Open up and move through the uncomfortable places in yourself that would keep you alone. Find a spiritual community that feeds your soul, and support it with your time, talents, and resources.

The journey of lasting transformation is quite a ride, as we peel away and let go of our perceptions of separateness and awaken to our Higher Self. I ran across this anonymous poem recently that made me laugh and think—two great experiences when done together, by the way.

> *Life is not meant to be a journey to the grave*
> *With the intention of arriving safely*
> *In a pretty and well-preserved body,*
> *But rather, we are invited to skid in broadside,*
> *Thoroughly used up, totally worn out,*
> *And proudly proclaiming,*
> *"Wow, What a Ride!!!"*

We are more than our stories, our histories, and the roles we play

When we make a conscious decision to awaken to that clear and more wholly essential part of who we are, the process set in motion has a tendency to reveal in us where the baggage is holding us back so that we can release it, lighten up, and reveal more of our Divine magnificence. That Divine magnificence is who we truly are. *We are more than our stories, our histories, and the roles we play.*

Something more than mere survival is calling you. Something more juicy, spicy, creative, and vibrant wants to be known in you. Something more restful, loving, and peaceful is calling to you in the deep, quiet recesses of your mind and heart. Can you hear it? It wants to emerge. Coded within you is everything needed for this emergence. However, this something must be called forth and ***you must empower its awakening***.

Let go of the small voice of limitation and bondage and choose to remember who you are. The power of repetition will be the practice that can shift you, your beliefs, and your experiences. Let go of the little voice of *Why did this happen to me again?* Stand tall and strong as the empowered spiritual being that you are! Again and again, we are re-presenting the Divine to Itself, until that day when the remembering is complete. Join me as we journey into this Reality, whole and free.

> *For as the Father hath life in himself; so hath he given to the Son to have life in himself.*
> *—John 5:26*

The following are affirmations that you can use as a template to create your own sleep-learning tapes or CDs. Simply use whatever parts fit your needs and speak them into your recording equipment. They can also be read daily to remind you of higher truths. If you prefer to purchase ready-made sleep-learning CDs, you may contact me at my website: www.janettemariefreeman.com

AFFIRMATIONS

I Rest and Go to Sleep Easily

- I am so relaxed and peaceful right now.
- As I lay down to rest, I feel my body relax and I am at peace.
- I am ready to go to sleep, and I know as I go to sleep that my body gets all the rest it needs.
- As my body sleeps, it is renewed and blessed and I wake up in the morning feeling great.
- My body rests perfectly and I am at peace.
- I am so tired now, and I am happy to rest and relax and go to sleep.
- It feels so good to cuddle up in bed and I feel safe and relaxed.
- I go to sleep easily now and I rest peacefully.
- I am ready to have peaceful dreams that rock me gently to sleep.
- I am safe and protected in every way.
- I feel so safe, so relaxed, and so protected.
- I am always safe. I have a wonderful and peaceful sleep.
- I am so tired and I am so relaxed.
- I know that as my body sleeps and rests, I can receive these sweet and wonderful messages.
- I accept these messages even though I am falling asleep.
- Even as I hear these words, they soothe me gently and I rest.
- As I hear these soft words, they are rocking me to sleep.

Reprogramming the Mind

- I will sleep soundly, but in the morning I will remember what I have heard.
- I am totally receptive to this new conditioning.
- Tonight I feed my subconscious new information. I want to hear these messages and I intend to integrate them into my life.
- I am letting go of my unsupportive belief systems and reprogramming me for health, success, love, and prosperity.
- These new beliefs are now creating the reality I desire.
- The words that I hear positively influence my subconscious mind while I sleep.
- The affirmations that I hear are now creating thought habits that will guide me to my desired objectives easily and effortlessly.
- Today I am using 100% of my mind's capacity.
- I now have easy access to the information in my subconscious.
- All subconscious information is being revealed to me now.
- I sleep restfully and easily.
- I am resting peacefully; every muscle in my body is relaxing.
- I sleep through the night resting in way that supports my body.

I Live in a Healthy, Loving Relationship

- All my relationships are richly supplied and abundantly blessed.
- My relationships enrich my life with joy and feelings of warmth and love.
- Love is abundantly supplied in me, because my very nature is love, and I give and receive love with ease and grace.
- My family and friends are abundantly blessed and they enrich my life in innumerable ways.
- I deserve love and open myself up to love in rich and wonderful ways.
- I do not run from love but I open myself to love in deep and meaningful ways.
- I can trust [men/women] because I can trust myself.
- I easily treat myself and everyone else with love and respect.
- I have healthy boundaries, giving and receiving in life.
- I am open to love and love is open to me.
- All of my relationships are a blessing to me.
- I accept all gifts that my relationships bring, even if they appear to be painful.
- I easily learn to love, share, and grow in relationship.
- I choose love. I choose to perceive love, and I choose to see the good in others.
- Nothing anyone does is about me; it is about them.
- I let others have their own life and I have mine.

- I am clear and I am complete in who I am.
- I trust life and I trust relationships.
- I find the love that I seek within myself and I and others are blessed.
- I allow others to have their own experiences.
- I am love and only love.

I Am Healthy

- I know that as I sleep, my body is getting healthier and healthier.
- My body always takes care of itself perfectly, always bringing about balance and health.
- My body always knows how to maintain perfect health.
- Every part of my body is held in the light and is perfect and whole in every way.
- I am so grateful for my healthy, strong body.
- I give thanks for my healthy, strong body and I give thanks that my body is always protected.
- All that I need to maintain health is available to me.
- My body is a rich resource of cells and nutrients that provide me all that I need to live a healthy life.
- My body is richly supplied with all that it needs.
- My body always seeks to restore balance.
- My body always heals, restores, and balances itself.
- I maintain healthy attitudes in mind and body.
- My body easily lets go of germs holds on only to what it does need.
- My body is intelligent, it knows exactly how to take care of itself.
- My body works perfectly. I am so grateful for my beautiful body.
- This moment and every moment my body responds to my call for greater health and wholeness.
- I am healthy.

Healthy Weight and Lifestyle

- My body easily maintains its perfect weight.
- I release all need to hold onto excess weight.
- I release all need to hold onto fearful emotions. I am safe.
- I surrender to my body's perfect expression and trust it fully.
- My body serves me beautifully.
- I no longer criticize or condemn my body and I accept it now completely.
- I know that my body's job is to seek balance and wholeness and I allow it to do so.
- My body finds its perfect weight.
- I let go of all beliefs that hold me in excess weight and I claim my strong, healthy, attractive body now.
- My body easily releases its excess weight.
- All desire for unhealthy foods is removed from me now.
- I choose to eat foods that nourish and support this body.
- I love eating in healthy ways.
- I love moving my body in ways that are perfect for me through exercise, sports, or other activities.
- I balance my movement with my intake of food, naturally and easily.
- I choose to eat, exercise, and maintain a healthy lifestyle.
- I make healthy lifestyle choices that support my healthy body and mind.

I Heal all Limiting Beliefs Around Money and All Supply

- Right now, I simply let go of all beliefs that no longer serve me in regards to my relationship to money. I love money and money loves me. I am a money magnet.

- I easily attract money and it comes in and out of my life with no stress or strain.

- I let go of all beliefs that say it is hard to have money. Money comes to me easily. Money comes to me easily and effortlessly.

- I am guided to great prospering ideas that manifest perfectly. I allow myself to receive money and let go of all limiting beliefs that would block it. I am a great receiver.

- I deserve to receive, and know and claim that I am worthy of receiving in all ways. I am prospered and blessed. That is my destiny.

- I let go of all limiting beliefs and I claim my abundant inheritance now.

- I am willing to receive the good that Life has to offer me and I claim it now.

- I am a great receiver. All good flows easily and effortlessly my way. I am prospered and blessed and I am willing to receive.

- I know that I am a good giver and I also claim that I am a good receiver as well.

- I am a money magnet. All good flows to me easily and effortlessly and I am so grateful to receive.

- I give thanks for the abundant good that prospers me in all ways. I receive easily and I give easily from the unlimited source of the abundant universe.
- I trust life to support me abundantly in every way as I give my gifts in joyful expectancy.

I See an Abundant Universe

- Everywhere I go, everything I do, I am keenly aware of the abundance all around me. I am in awe of nature's abundance.
- I see the way nature provides abundantly for itself and I am also a part of this grand nature.
- I see abundance in the ocean, the forests, the sky and all around me. I am embraced in abundance. I come from abundance and I return to abundance.
- I was created out of the abundant nature of the Universe and I open my eyes to abundance all around me.
- I am filled with joy and gratitude as I see all around me, moment by moment, the abundant nature of beauty, supply, sustenance, and rich prosperity.
- My eyes are opened to the abundant life all around me. My eyes are opened to the rich resources all around me. I see abundance. I experience abundance. I witness abundance. I am one with abundance.
- I could never be separated from abundance. I am rich with an attitude of abundance and I witness abundance all around me.
- I see beauty, joy, and prosperity and claim it for all people everywhere. I believe in rich resources, I experience rich resources, I live in rich resources and I can never be separated from this limitless supply. I know it for myself and I know it for others.

I Make Decisions

- I always trust my ability to make wise decisions.
- I let myself off the hook when I feel I may not have made great decisions.
- I learn from all decisions and I can easily make new ones.
- Moment by moment, I am making decisions that prosper, bless, and build others and myself.
- I trust my decisions and I let go of all fear about making them.
- I am guided and I do the best I can.
- I allow myself to learn, grow, make decisions, choose, and choose again when necessary.
- I make decisions knowing that the Universe is supporting my prospering good and I cannot make any mistakes that would cause harm to me or others.
- I am intuitively guided, creatively blessed, and abundantly prospered.

I Am Creative

- My mind is always open to new ideas that prosper and bless both others and me.
- Great creative ideas are available to me now.
- All my challenges are solved because of my creative thinking skills and my ability to tap into Universal Intelligence.
- I am a creative being full of great ideas that prosper and bless both others and me.
- There is no limit to the creativity in me, there is no limit to what I can see and imagine.
- My world of creative imagination is rich and alive. I no longer block myself. I am open up to the infinite source of divine ideas.
- I imagine and see vividly great new ideas.
- All that I need to know is revealed to me in perfect right timing.
- All knowledge, all wisdom, all guidance is available to me.
- I live and move and have my being in the expansive source of all truth, and Infinite Intelligence.
- I realize my oneness with Infinite Intelligence and I easily tap into this source for all that I need.
- I am creative and full of infinite life and infinite potential.
- I tap into that field of infinite possibilities and know that within that infinite field is all knowledge and wisdom.
- I tap into this field of infinite possibility and easily attract what is needed. I easily manifest my desires.

- I know that there is a Supreme Creative Intelligence that I can tap into easily. This Intelligence has all the answers, ideas, or solutions that I may need.
- I easily turn on the spicket to new information, knowledge, or guidance.
- I have an automatic guidance system that is working easily in and through me.
- I am guided day by day by this Creative Intelligence and It always guides me to a perfect course of action.
- I can trust Divine Intelligence, and I rely upon this Source rather than relying on the fears of the past, or the opinions of others.
- I trust myself and I trust the guidance that is within me.
- I live in perfect guidance, with a perfect guidance system.
- I trust myself, and I honor myself, and I give myself permission to make mistakes.
- I give myself permission to be guided moment by moment.
- I live in an acceptance of my guidance, my intuition, and myself.
- I trust the quiet voice within me to guide me, and I live in peace.

Trust

- I trust life in all ways and know that I am supported and sustained in every way.
- I let go of my need to control, manipulate, and change the world.
- I trust life to unfold easily and effortlessly in supportive ways.
- I trust life in all ways.
- I rest in the knowing that I am blessed, supported, protected, and sustained in all ways.
- I am abundantly supplied in this life with everything that I need.
- My life is a blessing and I let go of every idea that argues with this truth.
- I can never be alone for I am one with the Universal Nature of the all good and this Creative Intelligence is at work, in and through me in all ways.
- I can never be alone, I can never be without, I can never be lonely, and I can never be separated from my good.
- My good and me are interwoven, interconnected, and I am grateful to know that I am one with this Universal Life of all-knowing wisdom, support, light, and love.
- I trust life. Life trusts me. I live life in trust and absolute confidence.
- I trust life.

FOR CHILDREN...
OR FOR THE CHILD IN YOU...

I Am Loved

- I am happy that I am loved so much.
- I am a lovable person.
- Everything about me is lovable.
- I am surrounded by people who love and respect me.
- I am worthy of love.
- I am worthy of love in every way.
- I am so happy to be so loved and to be given what I need.
- I am a valuable person and I have a lot to share and a reason for being here.
- I am an important person.
- My feelings are important and my thoughts are important.
- I share my feelings and thoughts easily. I am loved. God is love and so am I.

Safety and Well-Being

- I am at peace because I am always safe.
- Whether I am at school, playing with my friends, or doing anything at all, I am always safe.
- I am surrounded in Light, which protects me in all ways.
- Nothing but good comes to me.
- I am always safe and I am always protected.
- Help is always available to me.
- I am safe and protected in every way.
- God protects me and blesses me all the time.
- Nothing but good comes to me. I always feel safe and secure because I am always protected and I am always provided for.
- I am safe in this universe.
- This universe is a safe place for me to live.
- I always trust that I am cared for, I am provided for, I am protected, and I am blessed.
- I live a blessed life. As God's beloved child, all things are blessing me and supporting me. I am so grateful to know this.

I Am Intelligent

- I am very smart.
- My mind is bright and I do well in my school work.
- I am smart because I know that there is a smart voice inside of me that is always helping me.
- My mind works well and I trust it.
- I can read easily and study easily and I remember what I study.
- I am peaceful in my school work and I trust and love myself.
- I do the best I can and that is enough.
- God is intelligent and so am I.
- I know whatever I need to know.

I Am Confident

- I am confident and secure that I am a wonderful person.
- I have a lot to share with others and I am confident.
- When I have something to say, I say what is on my mind with confidence.
- I don't need to be shy or worried about what other's think of me; I trust myself.
- I don't judge myself by what others might think; I am confident in who I am.

READING LIST

Live the Life You Love in Spirit, Co-authors include, Dr. Wayne Dyer, Deepak Chopra, Janette Marie Freeman and others, Little Seed Publishing

The Handbook to Higher Consciousness, Ken Keyes, Love Line Books (out of print)

There's a Whole in My Sidewalk, Portia Nelson, Beyond Words Publishing

Your Sacred Self, Dr. Wayne Dyer, Harper Collins

Power of Intention, Dr. Wayne Dyer, Hay House

The Spontaneous Fulfillment of Desire, Deepak Chopra, Harmony Books

The Science of Mind Textbook, Ernest Holmes, G.P. Putnam and Sons,

12 Conditions of a Miracle, Dr. Todd Michaels, Tarcher Penguin

Psychocybernetics, Maxwell Maltz, Simon & Schuster

The Man Who Tapped the Secrets of the Universe, Glenn Clark

Dare to Be Great, Terry Cole Whittaker, Tarcher Putnam

The Art of Being: 101 Ways To Practice Purpose In Your Life, Dr. Dennis Merritt Jones, New Reality Press

Building Your Field of Dreams, Mary Manin Morrisey, Bantam Books

A Master Guide to Meditation and Spiritual Growth, Roy Eugene Davis, CSA Press

ABOUT THE AUTHOR

Dr. Janette Marie Freeman's own transformation took her from a scared and lonely single mother of three, to an ordained minister, dynamic teacher, author, and president of a national organization. This transformation came about through the repetitive practice of spiritual principles. Thousands have already benefited from her down-to-earth style and inherent wisdom.

She has been teaching meditation, personal & spiritual growth for nearly 20 years and has a Doctorate in Consciousness Studies. As an author, speaker, teacher, minister and coach, she assists the person in moving through previous subconscious blocks in order to live more from their Higher Self and experience greater health, success, happiness and inner peace.

She founded two and served three spiritual communities as their minister and the spiritual director. She now serves a global community as an author, speaker, teacher, and coach and creator of meditations and online programs through Insight Timer, Breethe, and other online educational platforms.

She has created recorded programs to help reprogram the subconscious mind, assist with meditation and mindfulness practices and create transformation for over 10 years. Her programs are powerful and transformative and can be found on www.janettefreeman.com

Her vision and mission are simply to manifest more 'Heaven on Earth,' through a shift in consciousness individually and globally.

For information regarding seminars, workshops, or speaking engagements:

www.janettefreeman.com

Dr. Freeman is a dynamic, inspirational, and motivational speaker and can be contacted for speaking engagements.

Podcast: Soul Soup- "Food for your soul, and warmth for your heart"

Facebook https://www.facebook.com/Janettemfreeman/

Instagram@janette_freeman

Twitter @revnette

You Tube Dr. Janette Marie Freeman

Insight Timer Meditation App and Breethe Meditation App

CPSIA information can be obtained
at www.ICGtesting.com
Printed in the USA
LVHW040732181119
637663LV00002B/524

9 781983 838590